Other titles in the UWAP Poetry series (established 2016)

Our Lady of the Fence Post by J. H. Crone

Border Security by Bruce Dawe

Melbourne Journal by Alan Loney

Star Struck by David McCooey

Dark Convicts by Judy Johnson

Rallying by Quinn Eades

Flute of Milk by Susan Fealy

A Personal History of Vision by Luke Fischer

Snake Like Charms by Amanda Joy

Charlie Twirl by Alan Gould

Afloat in Light by David Adès

Communists Like Us by John Falzon

Hush by Dominique Hecq

Preparations for Departure by Nathanael O'Reilly

The Tiny Museums by Carolyn Abbs

Chromatic by Paul Munden

Fingertip of the Tongue by Sarah Rice

The Criminal Re-Register

Ross Gibson

Ross Gibson is Centenary Professor in Creative and Cultural Research at the University of Canberra. His work spans several media and disciplines. Recent projects include the Radio National feature program 'Green Love' (2016), the books *The Summer Exercises* (2009), *26 Views of the Starburst World* (2012), *Changescapes* (2015) and *Memoryscopes* (2015), all published by UWA Publishing, and the public-art installation 'Bluster-Town' at Wynyard-Baragaroo concourse, Sydney (2017).

Ross Gibson
The Criminal Re-Register

First published in 2017 by
UWA Publishing
Crawley, Western Australia 6009
www.uwap.uwa.edu.au

UWAP is an imprint of UWA Publishing
a division of The University of Western Australia

This book is copyright. Apart from any fair dealing
for the purpose of private study, research, criticism
or review, as permitted under the *Copyright Act 1968*,
no part may be reproduced by any process without
written permission.
Enquiries should be made to the publisher.

Copyright © Ross Gibson 2017
The moral right of the author has been asserted.

National Library of Australia
Cataloguing-in-Publication entry:
Gibson, Ross, 1956- author.
The criminal re-register / Ross Gibson.
ISBN: 9781742589558 (paperback)
Criminals—Poetry.
Criminals—Punishment—Australia—Poetry.
Sydney (N.S.W.)—History—Poetry.
Australian poetry—20th century.

Designed by Becky Chilcott, Chil3
Typeset in Lyon Text by Lasertype
Printed by Lightning Source

This project has been assisted by the Australian
Government through the Australia Council, its arts
funding and advisory body.

 uwapublishing

Gazetted

Throughout the twentieth century the Police Force in Sydney compiled a fortnightly gazette of paragraphs and photographs that anatomised local criminals and their escapades. Month after month the file would thicken until, at the start of every summer, the Government Printer gathered the previous year's paperwork into a 400-page almanac. Hardcover. Foolscap. Brought to book during December, the great sheaf of pamphlets became that year's *Criminal Register*. Each new edition was momentous, comprehensive, steeped in whatever moods and manias were then tingeing the town.

Every Police Station received the *Register*. Working with it in much the same way password-protected databases are used today, officers cross-referenced the fresh edition against archived relics. Chockablock with events and characters, divulging the argot and ideology of the year gone by, the *Register* offered rules, definitions and helpful hints. It listed names, *modi operandi*, distinguishing marks and traits of miscreants and lurk merchants fossicking in the underworld.

Decade by decade, this is what the anonymous editors of *The Register* called the criminal realm: 'the underworld'.

The underworld and its overlords, how ingenious and energetic both sides could be. What brutes they could be too, day after day, as they tracked and tricked each other, as they made and needed each other. The *Registers* reveal all this. There is some Dickens, some Dostoevsky, some DeLillo in every edition. Christina Stead, Kenneth Slessor, Arthur Stace and Ruth Park dwell in there too.

Not many *Registers* escaped custody to be appreciated by ordinary citizens. Police held their copies close. They were legally obliged to do so. I found my treasure ten years ago, along with a brown envelope full of unlabeled and undated photographic portraits, in a Kogarah junk-shop. The photographs dallied in a different part of the shop but even as they hid in anonymity, I felt they wanted to go with the big book.

So now I have this loose 1957 *Register*. For fifty years, it floated toward me. Since fastening on to it, enthralled, I've preserved it and mulled over it.

Now I've messed with it, overwriting original texts, reducing its bulk, altering names and addresses, treating it as a sketching-frame to fashion a slimmer fictional thing from its measurements and facts. As I've selected from thousands of *modi operandi* summaries, police procedures and malefactor-profiles, I've ransacked it to concoct a brew of found and forged prose-poetry, twisting it cack-handed to discern anew its themes, locales and characters so we might know humanity in some fresh way, in this present future that the fates have cast the prescient old *Register* into. And for all my meddling, plainly, I've never stopped revering it.

Here then is my re-mix of the renegade *Register*. Selectively I've pulled focus to the tough arc of beats that detectives called 'the horseshoe': from Tempe and Marrickville in Sydney's inner-west around the harbour-shores of Balmain, Glebe and Pyrmont, past Ultimo through the City proper out to Surry Hills, Kings Cross and Bondi in the near east. A psycho-geographic survey drawn from the heart of last century.

1957 – at the heart of last century – was a disturbing year in Sydney. Accelerated and vibrant. Cars started chewing the town. Further south in Melbourne, Australia's first Olympic Games had come and gone. The world had come and gone. TV had come and stayed. Which meant that odd new imitations of life were now soaking the town too. Mainly from a newly fabulated America. Mixed with some pickled BBC England. Plus a small but potent smear of the local vernacular. Music flooded in too, electric, fast and loud as throngs took to the stadiums, raddled with liquor and new drugs. Young people wanted the world and were saying so in a shout.

It was a big time, with a good dose of dumb and ugly mixed into some marvellous. A time that whelped the lustrous town – sprawling and brawling – that we stumble through now.

Who You will Find Here

Sham company boosters

                Hollow share hawkers

Coppers bent and unbent

                Grafters and verbalers

Backroom abortionists

                Dead body disturbers

Infant abandoners

                Men loitering in yards

Car thieves and motor strippers

                Mendacious women importuning on telephones

Club and concert-hall breakers

                Predators of reputation

Traffickers of minors

                Butchers unlicenced

Women cooking with chemicals

                      Purveyors of poorly provenanced smallgoods

Covert-camera seducers & follow-up extortionists

                                    Bushwhackers and Water rats

Merchant-navy ship-jumpers, especially Latvians and Hungarymen

                    Indecent exposers alarming minors and maidens

Bogus hotel usefuls

               Mutual abusers in gents' rest-rooms and undercrofts

Bordello-keepers in suburbs

                                      Dance-palace lotharios

Race-carnival dodgers, pick-pockets and cockatoos

                                          Pawn-shop stub-hustlers

Flophouse 'barbers' and 'buttermen'

Boarding-school snow-droppers

Hospital potion concocters and unguent filchers

Razzling theatre impresarios

Itinerant cads offering false assistance to the blind, halt and lame

Coat-hanger surgeons

Mashers and bashers

Cat burglars

Kiddy fiddlers

Book riggers and form fluffers

Shop lifters

House breakers

                        Pet stranglers

    Forgers & utterers

                    Railway thieves

                            Army absenters and Navy bailers

    Flash pitchers of woo

                                Warehouse breakers
    Sleeper train creepers

                    Magsmen

    Change ringers

                                Rattler jumpers

    Debt doctors

                    Bail squibs

Safe cracksmen

        Spielers & appealers

Incendiarists

                Conspirators

Grafters

        Abductors

Rock spiders

                Bagsnatchers

Concealers and revealers

        Phone-book kidney-sluggers

Billiard barn shills

                        Gin-jockeys, Distillery spooks & Sly-grog grinders

Racing Dog rustlers, meddlers and dopers

                                    Bomb chemists

Mail fondlers

                 Perverts in unnatural yen

Card sharps and dice loaders

                           Birds of passage

Gunmen & knifemen

                              Razor artists

Smut mixers and shifters

Sham icebox mechanics & car motor quacks

Sideshow rouseabouts and two-penny rustlers

Receivers and disposers

Sneak thieves

Milk-money nibblers

Shoddy droppers

Boat duffers

Wire pullers

Stock diddlers

Chloroform slumber doctors

Nag nobblers.

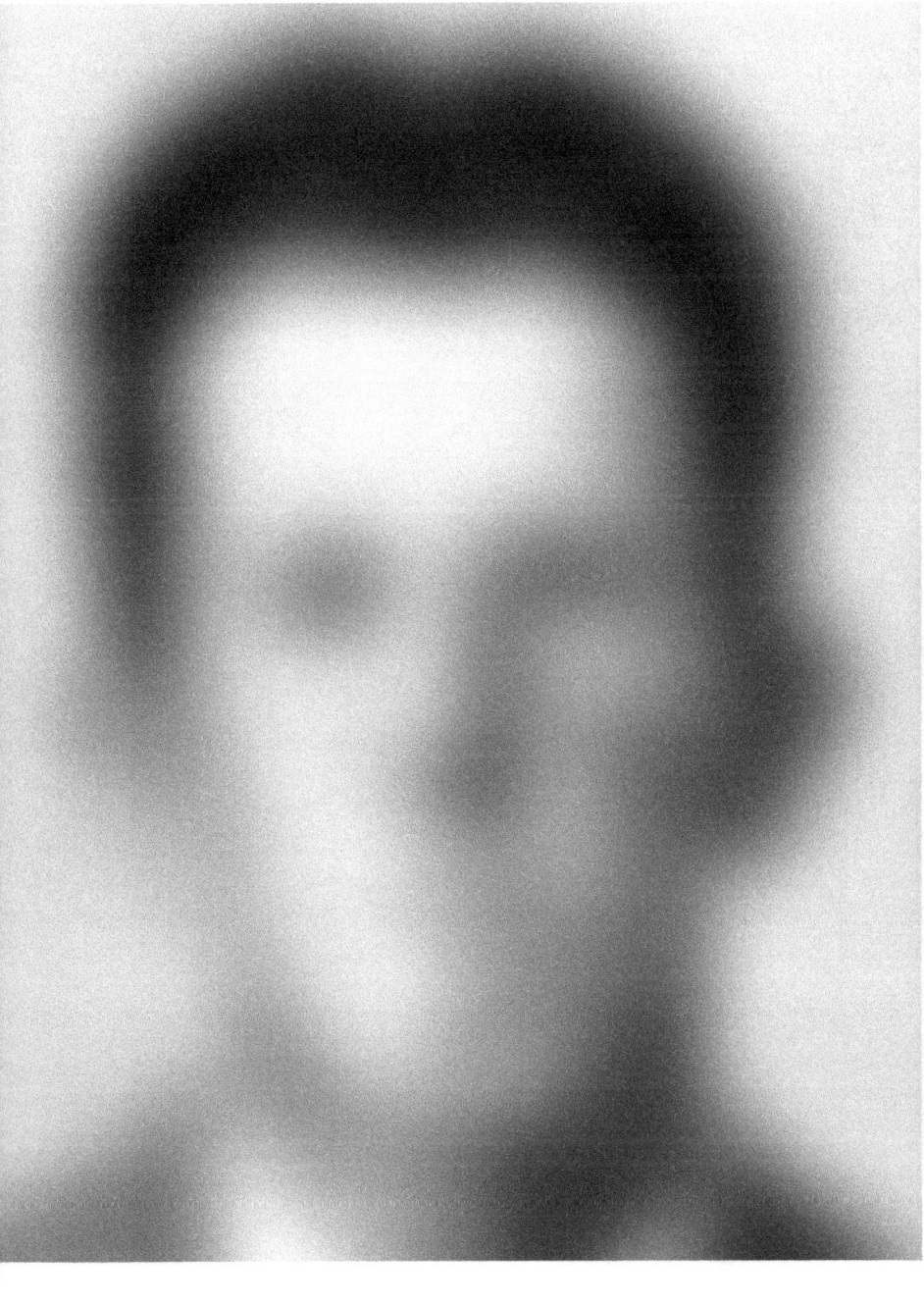

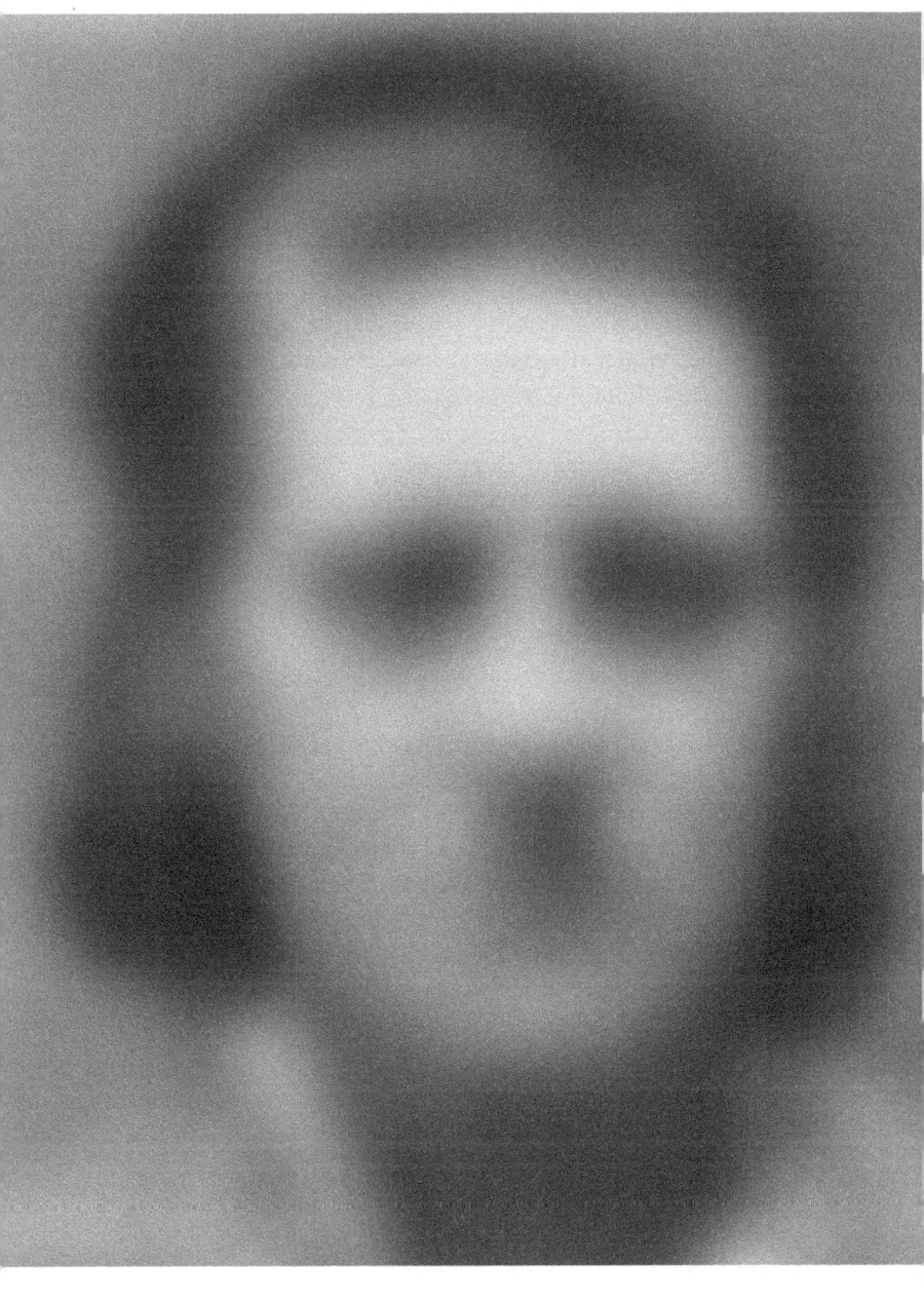

Notes for Detectives and Men in Plain Clothes

** Maintaining Intelligence:

    The Criminal Investigation Branch wants your best morsels of information.

    We need peculiarities, nick-names, apparent coincidences, subterfuges, ruses and tales told abroad, no matter how trifling they appear on first apperception. For who can tell which odd characteristic, picked from the sundry scintillas, might ignite a revelation from a pattern starkly lit up? A shopping-list can make a map to a mystery. A phone number or a shoe size will sometimes exonerate, sometimes incarcerate.

    Welcome every picture that you encounter. Now and then a lewd drawing will catch the eye of a judge. Do not dismiss or deplore such designs, no matter if they repel you. Learn to appreciate them, to assay them, to know their insinuations. For they might bring power to your prosecution.

    When you discover a name scrawled on a wall, accord it full, sober attention. Deduce if the author was right- or left-handed. Consider shooting a photograph.

    And remember: the best information is current information.

** The Office of Inquiry at Central Street Station is open and active twenty-four hours every day of the year. Because ditto the underworld.

** A long record exists (called, yes, "The Long Record"), that can be inspected at Central Street Station, preserving facts about every dead body that has been found in the town but has not yet been identified.

** Abandoned infants, live and dead: the same as above. Called "The Infant Record".

** Central Street Station keeps a Classified File of lost or stolen articles, encompassing many years. You might retrieve an article that was purloined long in the past as readily as one stolen two or three days ago. (Exception: the organic booty, susceptible to corruption, such as livestock or food. You must act on these promptly before your case rots down to stench.)

** When a jeweller repairs a watch, he will typically place his own secret mark faintly inside the back casing. Plus he tends to maintain a record of every customer seeking his service. A trove of the secret marks, representing most artisans in the State, is saved for your inspection at Central Street Station. But to scrutinize a *customer*-record, you must visit the jeweller and solicit his cooperation.

** There are cards in Central Street Records that classify the *modi operandi* of a full century of rogues. (Ask for "Indexed M.O.s.") Scrutinising these cards, attending also to the means by which the named felons were captured and convicted, you can find investigative inspiration and prompts for first actions when a fresh crime has been realized by newcomer miscreants. The cards are a store of longstanding police wisdom.

** Take this fact as a comfort: for the most part, there is nothing entirely new – no process, no shenanigan, no aspiration, anxiety or outrage – ever invented from scratch inside the underworld.

** Special books – "The Fatality Tomes" – are available at Central Street Station, holding all the statements and other notable utterances directly concerning *murders and manslaughters*. The Tomes date back uninterrupted to 1864.

** Inspect "The Occupation Cards" at Central Street Station. They list the "theatrical" or pretended roles criminals might play when committing misdemeanors: ship's captain, army officer, aviator, etcetera. The world is a stage, after all, and every life runs the course of some kind of drama. When a criminal cites an occupation as part of his story, most often he has previous knowledge of that very occupation, otherwise he leaves himself open to detection if defrauding a person who fortuitously grasps the occupation assumed. Note: do not be surprised when you find that such coincidences abound.

** This is a general rule: COINCIDENCES ABOUND.

** "The Peculiarity Cards" list the physical quirks of representative criminals: their tattoos, scars, deformities, gait, speech, tics, compulsions and so on. Become expert with these cards. These are in duplicate, with one set appended to "Modi Operandi".

** Approved summations of politically sensitive or notorious cases can be consulted in "The Public Interest Files". They offer guidelines. They are touchstones that indicate how the common people, and therefore our parliamentarian and ministerial masters devote their most ardent worries.

** Every Thursday, descriptions of the most flagrant current suspects are roneo-graphed on a high-priority sheet which is forwarded to every Detective and Plain Clothes Man in the city. Pluck this sheet from your piegieon-hole.

** Pay close attention to "The File of Suspicious Deaths". Sometimes you will see patterns there from the past that match well to the flow of the present.

** When stock are reported stolen or missing, the details are kept separate, under four classifications: Horses, Cattle, Sheep & Miscellaneous Beasts (including goats and prized working dogs as well as ferrets and pigs).

** Consider a perpetrator's "Trade Marks", such as traces of unusual acts committed at the crime scene, often unconsciously performed, sometimes compulsively so. For example: the consumption of peculiar foods or tobacco or hard liquor; the evacuation of bowels; ejaculatory stains; pulsations from puncture-wounds or the regurgitation of meals. Also: the cruel expungement of insects, the execution of pets, defilement of plants, the engraving of a brand in some intimate corner, or conversely in public view extravagantly bold. These foibles, tagged to particular perpetrators, are tabulated at

Central Street Station, in a file labeled "Trade Marks of Criminals". If cannily consulted, the file can lead to a conviction.

** All reports should be written LEGIBLY, with special care exercised regarding the correct spelling of names. No inscription is trivial.

** A card index is compiled of all persons who have been convicted or suspected of trafficking in the leathers of animals that are rare or protected. These cards are maintained and used chiefly by members of the Wool, Hide & Skin Squad. Put your request directly to the Head of the Squad.

** Each Detective must maintain and always have with him a Murder Bag. This satchel should bundle all the articles needed to investigate a homicide: measuring tapes and rulers, fingerprint outfits, at least one magnifying glass, several canvas screens and a trove of small but important incidentals such as pipettes, scalpel-knives, petroleum jelly and hermetically sealed jars that might secure sampled contents of intestines, a stool or a stomach. If in doubt, consult a Senior Detective to learn desiderata for the Bag.

** Know that a portable electric search-light is available for your use. Contact Central Street Station. Ask for the Quartermaster's Stores.

** Ground-to-air signal strips have been invented by the Rescue Intelligence Centre for use, should you need to arrest and guide the attention of an aircraft. Contact Central Street Station. Ask for the Quartermaster's Stores.

** Never hesitate to call on the expertise of the extraordinary men posted at the Circular Quay Sub-Station, gazetted under the name of The Police Shallow Water (Aqualung) Diving Squad.

** Consider the value of a plan-drawing. Ditto free-hand maps and rudimentary model-building. Ask your witnesses and suspects to put a story into whatever spaces you avail to them. Your imagined or modeled world might waft them back to the scene. (Accept but don't confess that this is just a rough kind of magic.) Invite witnesses and suspects to write and sketch all over your little worlds.
Give them pencils. Encourage the manifestation of gestures. And let your interlocutors make sounds, as if adding to a movie. Hark to much more than just character and plot. Sometimes an adjective or an adverb, a frustrated hand-flick, a sudden squint, a snort or an involuntary reiteration while 'doodling' with a pen can betray the whole composition of some malefactor's activities or entourage. Trust that careless words can be caught sometimes on the run. Attend to these words. Ditto an odd physical tic. Crucial clues often seek utterance despite the willful suppression forced by a cajoled witness or a dissembling perpetrator.

** At least one member of the Scientific Investigation Bureau is required to attend every scene of significant crime. He must cooperate with all investigating police to ensure that the technical examination of exhibits will generate utmost evidential cleanliness and prosecutional efficacy.

** Remember: conviction must brook no refutation or countervailing, and the judge and jury are lost to you unless you convince beyond quibble.

** In short, always be vigilant about Reasonable Doubt!

** At the scenes of homicides or suspicious deaths, a member of the Scientific Investigation Bureau, reporting perforce to the Superintendent of Detectives, must take charge of the scene and be responsible for photography and all necessary measurements before the body and related objects are disturbed. (See also the advice, already cited above, about the Murder Bag and its contents.) This SIB officer-in-charge will direct the search of the scene and environs, as well as the collection and preservation of exhibits and their continuous, assiduous examination and safe-keeping.

** Every man in the Scientific Investigation Bureau must maintain specified expertise: in the Library (for precision of memory); with the Technical Instruments Workshop (for divination and deduction); in the Document Compactus (for the fine analysis of language and the discernment of patterns in details) and in the Photographic Laboratory (for revelation and conviction).

** An index exists with the names and addresses of all professional men whose services you may beckon. "Services In-house". A Scientific Investigation Bureau detective is the go-between connecting these experts with the regular Police.

** Always strike a plaster cast of footprints, tyre tracks, jemmy marks and other impressions marking a scene. (Rubbing a lead pencil on white paper applied to a telling texture is also worth considering.)

** Technical analysis of exhibits may be conducted in the Central Street Laboratory, or by some trusted expert called in from outside the Police Force. Every thing taken away must be examined slowly and in fastidious detail. In the long run, secrecy among colleagues is not useful when bringing light to a mystery. "Sunlight is the best disinfectant". Everything occluded or mysterious should be brought explicitly into the investigators' view. For example, notice the space that has been left by the absence of a person or a thing from a scene. Something not there should still be seen as "a thing". Indeed, it might be the main thing.

** Summon the ultra-violet light whenever you sense it might help you. Its sepulchural hue can reveal an inscription on a faded tailor's mark, or make otherwise invisible stains explicit in cloth, leather or some other tell-tale surfaces. Remember: the occult can turn fluorescent under extra-spectral rays. The same goes for erasures and alterations in documents. What's thought to be gone can be roused from oblivion.

** Know all the transformations that can be visited on leather. And on metal, composition plastics, rubber and wood, particularly when these materials are components in: firearms, bicycles, tools of men's guilds, car and motor cycle engines, suit cases and handles, vehicle tyres and prestige or luxury goods. Understand how unauthorised processes can put changes in trade marks, lot numbers, monograms, stock insignias and brands. Once you notice the depredation, you might rouse apprehension and instigate rehabilitation, thereby retrieving the original information.

** High and low power microscopes and the experts who operate them are always at your disposal via Central Street Station. Ask at the Quartermaster's Stores.

** Aniline dyes and fluorescent powders are available for setting traps in cases of recurrent office theft. Also we have electrically operated buzzers and lamps and many types of concealed surveillance cameras.

** Alert a man from the Scientific Investigation Bureau if you encounter any technical problem arising in the detection and elucidation of a crime. Do not succumb to complacency. Inspect every scrape, scab or stain. Know the value of such traces. Every past action makes an impression. Everything tells something and nothing leaves nothing.

** Our Handwriting Section takes charge of all "Questionable Document Examinations", including the detection of erasures, alterations and forgery, plus the interrogation of hand-writing and type-writing on any printed matter. A man's hand can give him up; as can his machine.

** Experienced photographers are available in the Scientific Investigation Bureau. They can capture the image of any person charged with offences; or of a potential offender who is judged by officers as liable to lapse. Remember also that the camera is available to survey scenes of any crime, accident, fire, explosion, etcetera. Infra-red light and ultra violet procedures should also be considered, to enhance the photography in abstruse or unusual circumstances.

** Go to our specialists in forensics to understand firearms and bullets.

** Heed every exhortation in Police Instruction Number 27B77.

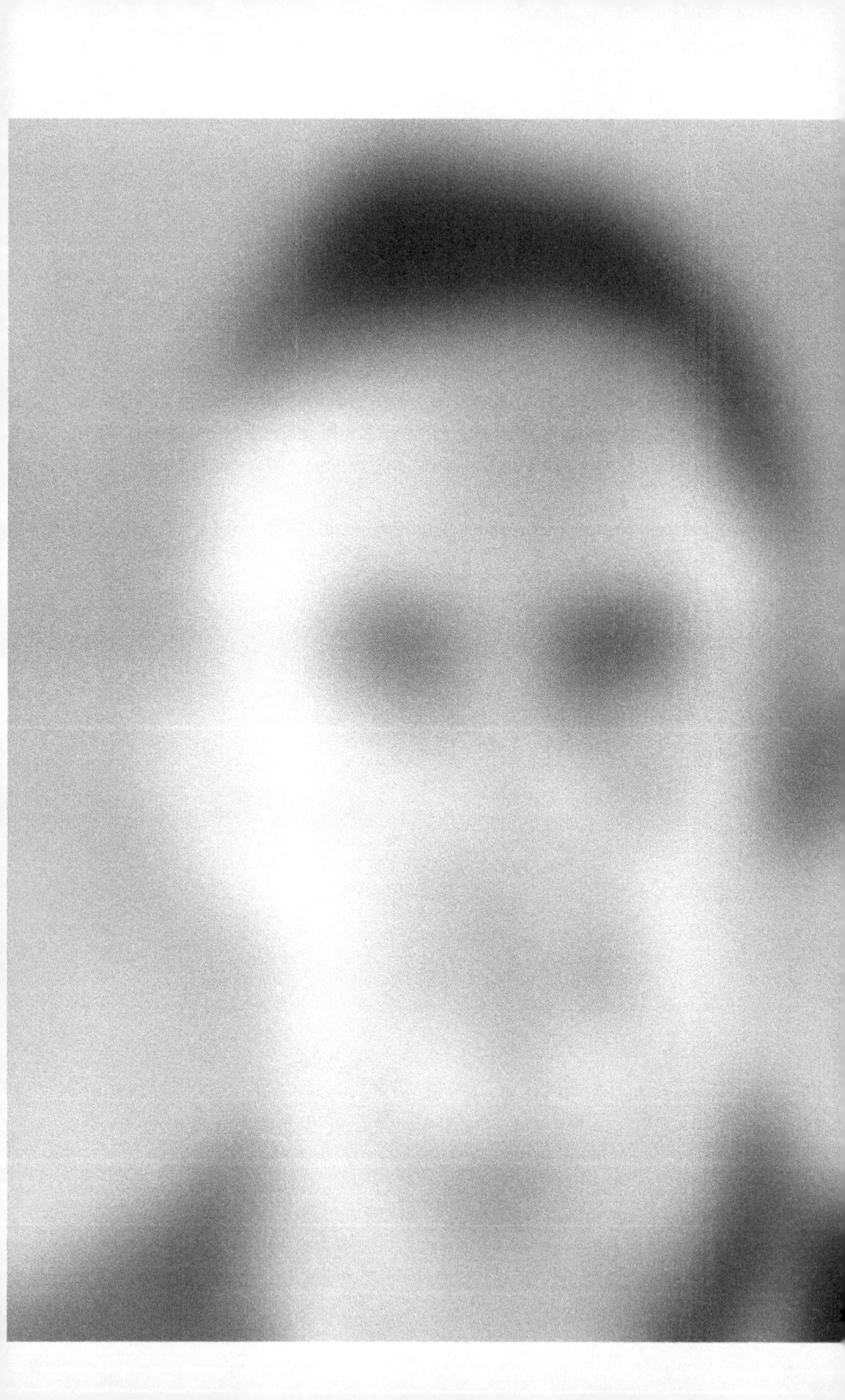

Underworld Nick-names and Noms-de-crime

William "Bodgy Bill" O'Connor

                Charles "Chooka" Chandler

Thomas "Smudge" Marks

                "Nurse" Emily Nightingale

"Bondi" Stan Merchison

                James "Mudgee" Farmer

Clarence "Chockablock" Chestnut

                Mervyn "The Keyman" Dawes

Lester "Legs" Walker

                Ah Kit "Sap" Ling

Ronald "Dummy" Waterhouse

                "Fingers" John Davis

Walter "Jockey" Gallup

                Kevin "Smut" Blacksnith

Patrick "Punchy Jack" Dempsey

"Side-lever" Sidney Wilson

Robert "Snorker" Ryan

Cyril "Squasher" McLean

"Stupid" Reg Smith

Edna "Squint" Corcoran

Sarah "Squat" Quartermaine

William "The Pelican" Waters

"Riverina" Ralph Shrives

Arthur "The Fairy" Wiseman

"Midnight" Peter Day

Albert Henry "Feathers" Weightman

"Ugly" Albert Pegley

"Pretty" Pete Pallister

Kevin "Slab" Banville

"Kangaroo" John Hopgood

"Bumper" Bob Biggs

                    "Excitement" George Exeter

"Easy" Esme Allison

                    William "Cosh" McIntosh

Frank Lee "The Flea"

                    Niccoli "Nerves" Agroponte

Timothy "Stink" Theodore

                    "Queen" Victoria Simms

Albert Arthur "Soot" Alabaster

                    Wallace "Chink" Westaway

James "The Whip" Smart

                    Herman "Pansy" Bloom

Sidney "Tackler" Madigan

                    Arthur "Cockeye Ben" Bennington

Neville "Nugget" Goldie

                    Robert Albert Hopkins, alias "Squirter"

Malcolm "Face" McLean

                              Mervyn "Slogger" Williams

Patrick Flannery, alias "Darkie Murphy"

                         Alfred "Cadger" Pound

Batholomew "Buster" Bannister

                         Edward "Boot Face" Smart

Cecil Chester Goddard, alias "The Target"

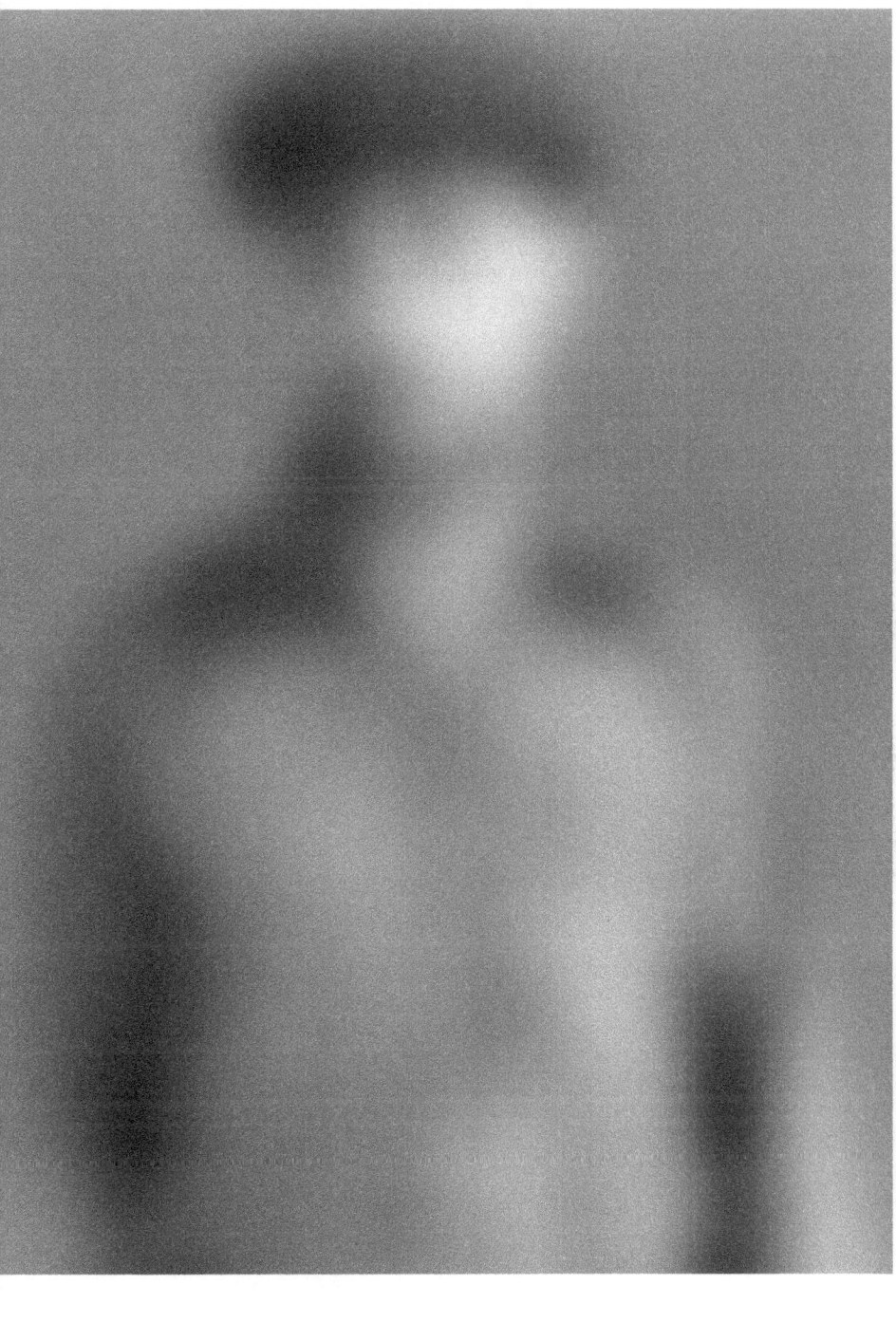

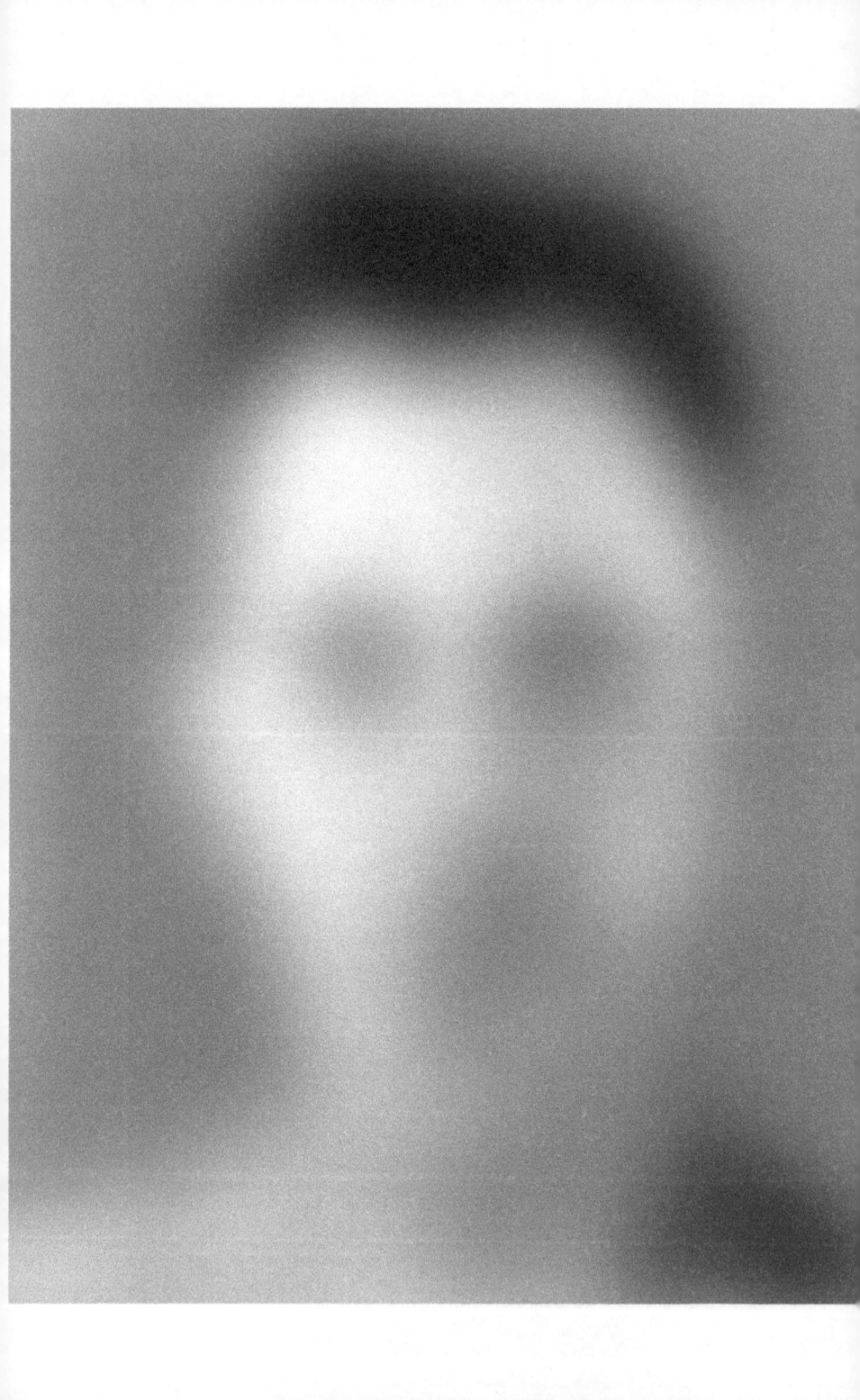

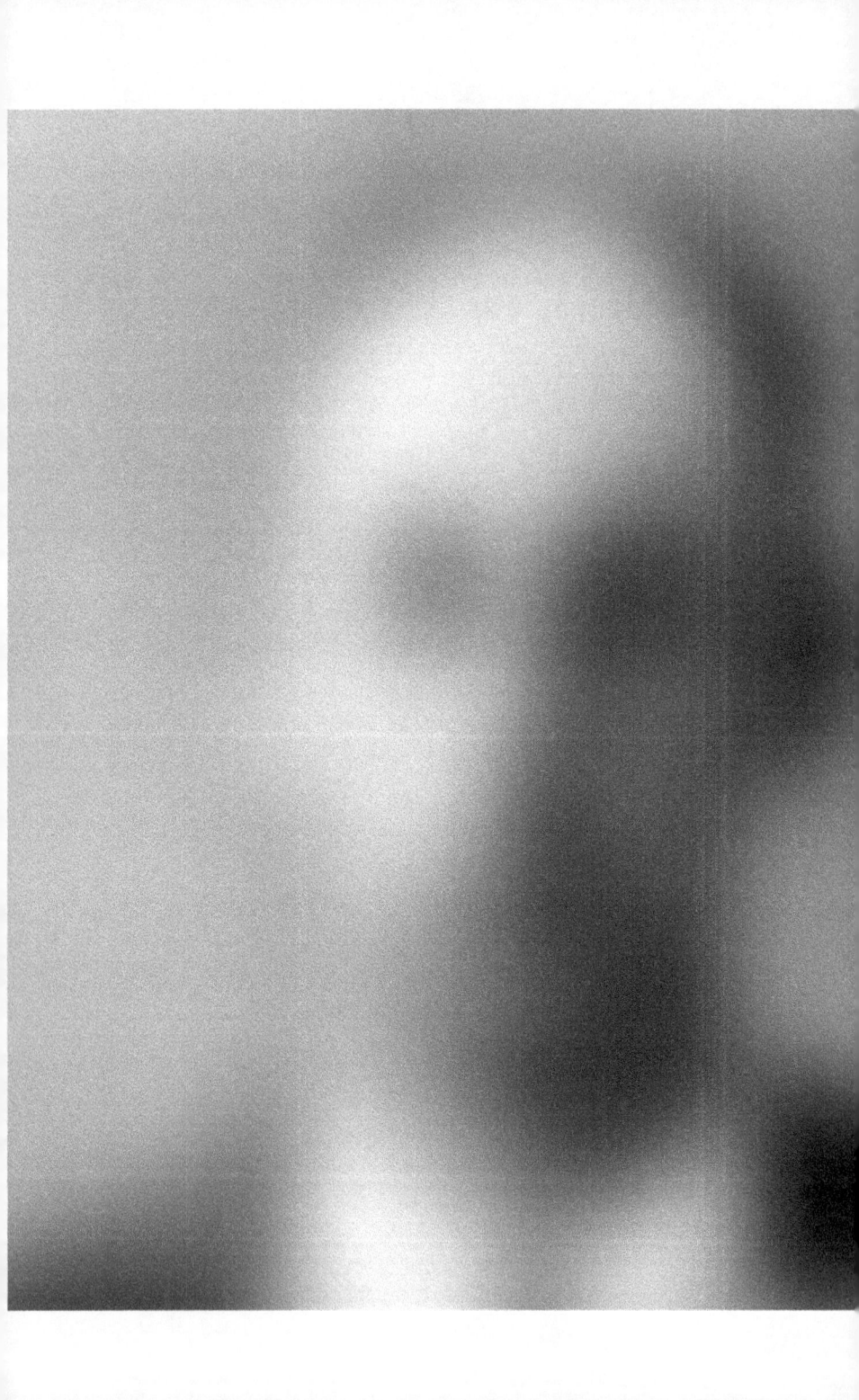

Modi Operandi & Malefactors' Marks of Distinction
(including tattoos, scars, traits, miens and gaits)

Ronald "Dummy" Waterhouse

5 feet 7 inches; 48 years; sallow complexion; hair thin and receding; dishwater grey eyes.

A large comma-shaped scar snarls soft skin under left wrist.

"Hope" and "Will" tattooed on left and right upper arms; a woman's head and "DELORES" printed backwards on chest.

Sometimes wears a scarlet handkerchief adorning the throat. Entirely deaf-and-dumb.
A native of Sydney. Ineffectual kitchen-hand & lackadaisical floor-mopper. Opportunist thief.

Case study:

>Manipulated the bolted door of a warehouse in lower Waterloo; took a large quantity of liquor.

>Retired to a gambler's den at Blackwattle Bay.

>Used a handwritten note there to try uttering the goods.

>Same note returned later to incriminate him in court.

Loiters with billiard shills in Newtown and The Haymarket.

David Oscar Bentham

5 ft 10 in; sun-blotched complexion; hair ginger & curly but grey at the temples; rust-coloured smudges speckle green eyes.

Large scar from a burn on the back of head reaches down past a livid redness at the nape of the neck and between the shoulder blades; gunshot pepper-pod scars spay along the left arm; and bone-chip indentations disfigure the left ankle.

A heart pierced by an arrow, tattooed on right forearm

A native of England.

Claims to be director of a company in the city.

Often sports pencils in breast pocket, to give the impression he is a master of accounts. Is in fact a false promiser and inveterate pretender.

Case studies:

> Once approached a bank manager in Campsie, seeking a loan of 50 pounds to finance a play which he alleged to be ready for broadcast from a licenced radio station. (1949.)

In 1953 Offender resided with a family on a pastoral property west of WeeWaa. Purported to be Sir David Oscar Bentham, the latest Earl of Chelsea.

In the glow of his title, offender romanced and affianced a daughter and prevailed upon the family to sell the property and accompany him to England.

But the father intervened against the wishes of the daughter and reported offender to the Metropolitan Police.

"Sir David Bentham" promptly went missing. The daughter remembers his scars.

Months later: offender obtained employment as an accountant in a Pagewood film production company where he secured 500 pounds from two employees, showing his prospectus for a television company. Issued 2000 bogus shares to these investors, eliciting 200 more pounds, before absconding and vanishing.

A spinster secretary at the Pagewood company has provided descriptions of his scars.

She is embittered now and eager to tell.

Often wearing unentitled war medals and decorations, offender is cunning and appears suave and fully plausible.

Well-spoken.

Of quiet disposition.

Seldom wears a hat.

Percy Ronald Collister

5 ft 9 in; ruddy complexion; hair auburn and straight; pale blue in the eyes; voice queerly high pitched.

An angry red welt and a raised scar brand the centre of forehead; deformed elbow juts wrong from straightened right arm.

Dragon, flag and "Australia" tattooed on left bicep; thistle, clasped hands and "Bonnie Scotland" tattooed on right bicep; on the right forearm, a snake coiled around a stump.

A native of Glasgow, more recently residing in Corowa. Was dismissed from his role there as a wheat lumper and sheaf tosser. Decamped to Sydney.

House breaker and cat burglar.

Case studies:

> Travelled to Marrickville on a motor-bike stolen from a farm outside Queanbeyan.
>
> Ransacked vacant townhouses, enroute, in Moss Vale and Bundanoon.
>
> Apprehended in Enmore, recklessly driving, both paniers laden with jewellery, cutlery and damp cash.

On another occasion, when pursued by Police, offender joined a group of workmen nearby, shucked off his coat, picked up a hammer and commenced nailing palings to a fence.

Once apprised of the presence of the Police and what they were seeking, the offender's new "comrades" laid hands on the culprit and threw him at the paddy wagon.

Addicted to drink.

Cannot repel blandishments of dissolute associates.

Richard Lawrence Brass   alias **Richard Lawrence**
alias **Lawrence Anger**

42 years; 5 ft 11 in; solid build; florid complexion; ginger hair; green eyes, misted.

Large snake tattooed all along and around the left arm; scotch thistle inked on right forearm.

Native of Victoria; may be hiding in boarding-houses around the Sydney Harbour horseshoe.

Labourer.

Safebreaker and thief.

Case studies:

> In 1952, offender set a fire in the Royal National Park which finally stretched from Maianbar to Burning Palms, a full seven miles.
>
> One night in July 1954, prior to payday at Upper Ridge Construction Camp #2, outside Kosciuszko, offender travelled from Yass with Arnold Albert Ballantyne (see *Register* 1956), in a stolen red lorry, to the office of said camp.
>
> Entered office by forcing a window with a jemmy; carried away two safes holding £2,500.

(Vehicle was parked some distance away.)

Freighting the safes, the culprits were exposed, causing a melee amongst the camp-dwellers, forcing culprits to abandon the safes and decamp at high speed.

When several miles from the camp, culprits' lorry skidded on icy curves, forcing abandonment of vehicle and flight into scrubland.

Early next morning, betrayed by a fire they had set to gather warmth, culprits were apprehended at back of a damp cave.

Offender associates with notorious criminals in the capital cities of all states. Has extensive knowledge of explosives, which he puts to use for own enterprises as well as "hired orders" commissioned by other members of underworld. Payment is often a matter of violent dispute.

Recently released after three years hard labour in Goulburn jail.

Thought to be consorting with old running mates in The Haymarket and Bondi.

Alfred Percy   alias **Purdy**   alias **Frederick James Waddington**
alias **Alfred Percy Gilligan**   alias **Arthur Lamington**
alias **Alfred Arthur Lloyd**   alias **Albert Lord**

A native of Baradine; 5 ft 9 in; 43 years; powerful build; medium complexion; black hair and brown-black eyes.

Circular scar three inches in diameter on right upper buttock; a triangle around the capital letter "B", like a cattle brand, on upper left buttock;

Tattoo of a boxer on outside left upper arm, tattoo of a star on back of left hand, tattoo of clasped hands and heart with faint letters "DOA" in the centre of inside left forearm, anchor and cross above an anvil on inside right arm near armpit, daisy flowers on back of right hand.

A pugilist, once professional, now habitual as a stand-over man. A labourer.

Early 1955, offender was sentenced to eighteen months' hard labour on charges of break, enter & steal.

Recently released on license, term expired.

Case studies:

> Previously convicted in England, Western Australia, South Australia and Queensland on charges of stealing; being on premises with wherewithal and intention to steal; inflicting

grievous bodily harm; unlawful possession; escape from custody; breaking and entering a counting-house with intention to steal; stealing in a dwelling; loitering in a yard; assault police; assault prison guards.

May be lying low now in Darlinghurst; or decamped to country Victoria.

Roy Leslie Victor, alias **Dr Grant Opal**, alias **Jean-Pierre Gaumont**

33 years; 6 ft 0 in; pale in complexion; hair red and crinkled; smoky blue eyes. A dagger through the chest tattooed on left breast, directly on top of his heart. Erect carriage; takes short quick steps when walking outdoors.

60 per cent of the left index finger has been crookedly amputated, as if bitten and spat out.

Inclined to inflict bodily harm without provocation. Seeks the company of boys in parks and reserves, where he tell tales of his experiences and also tattoos their arms and legs.

Native of Granville.

Boot clicker and occasional bookmaker's ticketman and penciller. Pretender & embezzler; stand-over man; boarding-house "barber"

Case study:

> In the span of one hot summer's day, offender entered his father's home in Woollahra and stole clocks and a watch, a radio and a rifle. Then went into Paddington and gained a hotel room-key by false pretenses and carried off the suitcase of an unsuspecting tenant. Proceeded later to peddle his wares cheaply in an Ultimo boarding-house.

Finally was apprehended drunk and disorderly on the last ferry to Manly.

Thought to be subsisting at present by riding night-time rattlers to outlying suburbs. Sleeping on trains and in rail yards. Also seeking temporary accommodation and food on Hunter Valley farmland in exchange for oddjob labour.

Peter George Grange

31 years; a native of McDonaldtown; 5 ft 9 in; fresh complexion, brown hair and tan eyes; nose has been broken several times, often severely.

Door-to-door salesman.

House-breaker and ladies man. Recently released.

Case studies:

> On one occasion, whilst residing at parental home in Lewisham, offender forced a door on a wardrobe in his mother's bedroom, during her absence, and stole money, jewellery and cheques. Then took off for Melbourne. Left a note saying, "Sorry Mum. Love Peter."
>
> On another occasion, just as offender was leaving a dwelling which he had ransacked, the occupants returned home and offender fled undetected and went directly to a milk carter nearby who happened to be delivering his goods to the victims. Milk carter gladly accepted offender's kind offer of assistance. Offender was blithely serving customers in the vicinity when the Police officers arrived and subsequently departed, ineffectual. Offender declined offer of payment from carter.
>
> Once called on a woman in Balmain, stating he was a representative of the Saint Vincent de Paul Society. Asked

for an annual subscription, in return for which, victim would receive instructional pamphlets, prayer books, homilies and sermons as well as a powerful indulgence that would protect herself and her children from vice and all accidents of violence. On receiving the cash, offender gave victim a hand-coloured postcard depicting her Guardian Angel.

Travels by tram, bus or public conveyance to and from the scenes of his crimes, which typically occur in the outlying suburbs. Offender spends the proceeds of his activity on the races and frequenting holiday resorts with young women of easy virtue. (Whether his recent marriage, consummated immediately after latest liberation from prison, will curtail his indiscretions, remains to be seen.)

Of quiet disposition and pleasant manner; usually well dressed and of smart appearance, with his hair well oiled and parted on the left; is fond of dancing and frequents Miss Esme Richards' waltz studios in Sussex Street, Haymarket; also lurks in billiard rooms around Chippendale and the Central Rail Station.

Careless with fingerprints.

Michael Leslie Costigan

30 years; 5 ft 10 in; strong build, weighing in at 12 stone 8 pounds; swarthy complexion; dark brown crinkled hair; brown eyes under heavy brows; scarring on left eyebrow and under right eye; clean-shaven; high cheekbones within a long face. Usually wearing well-pressed navy-blue suit, a soft collared white shirt with silver cufflinks and red tie, felt hat and tan shoes.

"Molly" and "Nola" tattooed on left forearm; a forget-me-not, a bird, an anchor and "Edith" decorating right arm from bicep to wrist.

Pretender and forger.

Makes multiple applications for food relief and charitable donations, pretending to supply destitute families in Waterloo; sells false insurance policies door-to-door; telephone tale-teller.

Associates with rough types in The Haymarket. Ditto around Malabar.

Claims to be a retired boxer who once fought under the names of "Jolting" Joe Jespersen and Cedric "The Cyclone" Aspinall.

Oftentimes is accompanied by two sinister men who cannot be described better nor identified with current information.

Fernandez Rufalo   alias **Nicolo Papas**

39 years; 5 ft 9 in; thin build; dark complexion; black wavy hair brushed back across crown; clean shaven; thin, wrinkled face; speaks with an accent that he insists to be Spanish; wears horn-rimmed spectacles that give eyes a glassy look; rarely seen without a cigarette glowing in mouth.

Usually employed in Mediterranean-style cafes and restaurants and speaks the Greek language in a rudimentary fashion; boasts of his ability to invent and make cocktails.

False pretender and embezzler.

Case study:

> Claimed to have photos of the proprietor of a large City public house, photos of the man *in flagrante* with a woman not his wife; declined to show the pictures but extorted payment for their destruction. On the failure of this ruse, offender appears to have decamped to the Blue Mountains.

Last seen at Central Railway Station carrying a green canvas sack cinched with red twine. May be at large in Bathurst or points further west, or may have suffered a misadventure instigated by any one of the myriad reprobates he has antagonised in recent years.

Lisle Conor Jameson   alias **Louis James Conniston**

5 ft 8 in; fair complexion; hair grey & wavy; eyes a tarry brown that registers as black in sombre light.

Scar on centre of forehead, right wrist, each temple and along the left forearm; a bright surgical scar slashed in the right side of the abdomen.

Native of Ireland.

A rouseabout and farm labourer, offender was last year expelled from a property near Inverell.

Recently employed as a miscellaneous useful with the offices of the Post Master General in the City.

A fraud and dissembler.

Case study:

> Suspected of tampering with parcels when accompanying the mail-lorry from Sydney General Post Office to Central Train Station. In league with a local mail sorter, who isolated and identified one PMG satchel containing government bonds and cheques bound for the Bank of New South Wales, North Sydney Branch. On running the errand from GPO, neither the offender nor the satchel ever presented at Central or in North Sydney.

Walter Fraser Gallup   alias **"Jockey" Gallup**

5 ft 3 in; pallid complexion; hair brown and curly, receding and thin; eyes a frosty blue, crossed and ill-focused.

First knuckle missing on right index finger. Sickle-shaped scar on right upper clavicle. Cauliflower ears, both left and right.

Native of Cornwall. Motor mechanic.

Dismantler and distributor of ill-gotten machines.

Case study:

> Stole a Jeep off the street one sunny Surry Hills morning. Offered it for sale to the Hunter Valley County Council. (Had re-coloured the chassis with cheap brown enamel and distorted the engine number with rudimentary welding and etching.) When sedan was presented to prospective buyers, a moist mottle in the paintwork raised prompt suspicion.

A physical coward. Breaks composure when threatened verbally. No physical duress required. Will offer up accomplices before a hard hand is laid on him. Ten minutes alone in a dim cell primes him ready to squawk.

Amelia Beryl Martens

56 years; thin physique; nervous disposition; medium complexion, brown hair, hazel eyes.

A native of Guyra.

Claims to be a solicitor's clerk.

Recently released after serving five years' hard labour for manslaughter. Abortionist; manslaughterer.

Works in tandem with Robert Walter Abbott, an infamous abortionist falsely claiming the title of "Doctor". The two culprits have conspired since 1939.

Case study:

> Last arrest was occasioned by the death of a married woman due to massive haemorrhage, following an operation performed by both culprits at offender's home in Ultimo. Deceased had first called at Abbott's flat in Surry Hills; after examining her there, Abbott accompanied victim in a taxi to offender Martens' abode, where the fatal procedure occurred.
>
> In addition to the body, investigators discovered surgical implements at culprit's domicile. Plus, more tools of trade were secreted at Abbott's address.

(Alarm had been raised by an associate of the deceased, delivering police first to the bloody scene, then on to the accomplice's abode.)

Both malefactors denied any wrong-doing and claimed to be champions for women and servants of the poor.

Offender Martens is customarily well dressed, frequenting the city and the Harbour horseshoe of suburbs, soliciting new victims and consulting with the desperate.

Ditto the conspirator Abbott.

Leonard James Richards

17 years; 5 ft 8 in; complexion fair but mottled; hair fawn and fine and prone to be windblown; a pale blueness in the eyes gives appearance he is sunblind.

Volcano-shaped scar on right ankle; a broad scraped red lesion along left instep and up the inside of ankle; heavy suture marks from big toe to the back of the heel of right foot. 4-inch crescent welt plus a star, resembling a real cattle brand, on the inside upper right arm.

Native of Sydney. Apprentice blacksmith. Housebreaker, incendiarist and murderer.

Case study:

> Was engaged as a houseboy on a property near Guyra. In the frigid Central Highlands. Was left alone there to tend the needs of the owner's "difficult" son while owner and wife took a pleasure-trip to Sydney.
>
> On the first night of abandonment, offender claims he became lonely and frightened (he is seventeen years old). Subsequently found a rifle and revolver and caches of ammunition. Took solace from this booty. Conjured the idea of claiming these weapons, stealing employer's best vehicle, and absconding to Queensland. Decided on the new name he would go by, which he wrote on the label of a stolen tweed blazer: "James Richard Lonergan". Unespied by offender, however, employer's son

was secreted in the parlour of the homestead and therefrom watched offender lift and load the stolen rifle. On being startled by the son, who had exclaimed out of fear, offender shot the scared scion in the side of the neck. Victim wrested the weapon, beat offender about the head and then ran to the telephone where he called out the danger.

At this moment, offender recovered from concussion, deploying the revolver to shoot the son directly in the chest.

Victim staggered to the car shed where offender found him on hands and knees and in a state of collapse. Offender then fired three more shots into the wilting body and the back of the head.

Next, collected clothing (notably an Army greatcoat in which he would be subsequently apprehended), plus food and a small sum of cash secured in a leather pouch plucked from the unfortunate's stripped body.

(For police records only: Coroner noted confidentially that victim had undergone "more than only death".)

Prior to leaving the property, offender cut telephone wires, used a mattock to puncture all fuel tanks and deflate tyres under every vehicle on the farm.

At last he purloined and decamped in employer's Chevrolet saloon after shooting and setting fire to three black-and-white sheep dogs.

At the nadir of his misfortunes, after abject months avoiding arrest, offender was lost, starving and destitute in Woy Woy, where he entered the home of the local bank manager, ransacked the rooms and set fire to clothing.

Seemingly intent on detection in this chapter of his narrative – driven by foibles still to be understood by investigators – offender had boasted to regulars in the public bar at the Woy Woy Traveller's Rest, declaring he was due for an exciting rendezvous, night-time, in Kings Cross.

Hence his arrest three days later at sunrise, waving an empty revolver and inebriated by spirits, in a service-access lane in Elizabeth Bay.

Both feet were wrapped in hessian and twine at the time of apprehension.

Previously frequented the Alexandria environs, where he had no criminal associates and once tried out vainly for the Newtown youth rugby league team.

Arthur Ambrose Stiles

6 ft 2 in; freckled complexion; hair auburn and wavy; frosty blue eyes. Wears an Akubra town-hat of olive-hued straw.
Stooped and long-loping when striding down the street.

Two Y-shaped scars blaze pink on the right cheek. Four vaccination welts glow bright and angry on his outside left arm.

Native of Whyalla, in remote South Australia. An instrument-maker and a fine-detail etcher. Re-located into Sydney in 1954.

An embezzler and a thief.

Case study:

>Attained a position of trust as manager of the Watch Repair section in a Broadway emporium.
>
>On numerous occasions, offender returned to the store after hours, ostensibly diligent to work on a backlog of tasks. During each stealthy visit, however, he lifted articles from retail vitrines, articles such as jewellery, lingerie, several wrist-watches, one camera and an electric-powered razor.
>
>Some of this property became gifts to a lady friend; the remainder was converted to offender's own enjoyment.

Offender is of quiet disposition, sober habits, a dapper dresser, and keeps no known criminal associates. A neophyte thief, perhaps in thrall to a newly risen mania that cannot be tempered by his will.

Ardently attentive to nubile young women.

Albert Henry Weightman, nicknamed **"Feathers" Weightman**

5 ft 4 ½ in; complexion wan; hair dark & wavy; eyes a black sheen.

Nose, broken often, now spreads to one side; left ear is lobe-less; right ear is birth-marked bright red and mottled.

A native of Erskineville. Once a featherweight pugilist, fighting in stadiums under the nom-de-guerre "Antonio The Storm".

A tiler and lorry-driver.

A larcenist, receiver and transactor of ill-gotten goods.

Case study:

> Under the influence of liquor, took a black sedan from King Street in Newtown; drove it to Windsor; broke into an orchard; stole a large quantity of peaches.
>
> Apprehended at Wisemans Ferry with the back doors opened on the vehicle, selling produce stacked roof-high inside.
>
> Had disposed of very little: only the driver's compartment was free of vegetation.

Whilst offender has no robust mentality, he can be a bold liar. Compulsive.

An officer's best method is to prompt and keep offender talking until the fool is tripped and hoist by the complicating contradictions that he has previously bound into his gushed fabulation.

Noel Robert Bruce

5 ft 9 in; fair, pimpled complexion; hair brown, lank and long; olive-green in the eyes; protruding upper-jaw teeth; inclined to be hump-backed; walks with head down.

Woman in bathing costume wrapped about by a snake tattooed on left forearm; knife with red handle high on left upper arm; heart, scroll & "ESME" on right upper arm; "ESME-NOEL" on a banner inside the right forearm.

Native of Surry Hills.

Road labourer and hotel oddjobber. Metal thief and opportunist.

Case study:

> October 1956, offender travelled one night in a car owned by an unidentified accomplice. Visited a Woolloomooloo factory yard and stole a large number of lead ingots. This property was then melted in his Surry Hills home, cast into small portions, and availed to receivers in Annandale.
>
> Offender next broke into a warehouse via a canal track in Tempe where he stole a number of exotic machines, including a motor-driven bacon cutter, a stainless steel brisket slicer, outsized beast-toting scales, a caterer's juice extractor plus several large electrical vegetable mashers. Offender took these implements in a stolen lorry down to Wollongong where he

approached potential customers who raised suspicions once offender was exposed to be incapable of correctly operating the intricate assemblages. Left the lorry and equipment in the loading bay of the last premises and caught a train back toward Central.

Still roaming at large. May have jumped a rattler to Casino.

Was last known to reside in the Lord George Hotel in Upper Waterloo. Over any period of three months, offender will be without fixed abode most nights of each week.

Basil Keith Bainbridge

5 ft 7 in; fair complexion and hair; chalky blue in the eyes.

Star-shaped scar above the left temple; a perfectly round red burn mark, the size of a penny, on the neck below the left ear; walks quickly using short steps that are ragged like a stagger.

Native of Canterbury. Qualified solicitor.

Criminal Roles: embezzler and confidence trickster.

Case study:

> While operating as a solicitor in Chippendale, he was entrusted with sums of money from industrial clients, including MacRobertsons Famous Sweets, in payment for expediting transfers and subdivisions of land. Offender secreted these wherewithals in a camouflage escrow and decamped north to Brisbane, where he lived several months like a grandee in that volatile economy. There he inhabited bayside addresses under a clutch of assumed names, including "Septimus Clive Ormistead", "Major Thomas Mitchell" and "George Wellesley West".

Last known whereabouts: a canefield hotel in Far Northern Queensland.

Offender has a prodigious ability to perform British accents; also Canadian as well as Californian. Under what names he assumes these latter guises, the law is yet to ascertain.

Elijah Solomon Stein

5 ft 8 in; swarthy complexion; hair dark brown with grey pepper; eyes mottled hazel.

A question-mark scar curling beneath the left eye.

Speaks several languages and, though Jewish in parentage and appearance, offender is in fact a native of China. Intimate with Dixon Street Chinamen. Visits there in upstairs rooms and private smoking parlours.

In the habit of sucking his left thumb.

Was once interrogated in York Street by Central Street police for pretending to be a bus driver.

Storeman and stoke-loader for a George Street emporium. Novice car thief and stripper of engines.

Case study:

> While travelling half-inebriated in his car to a Castlecrag party, Stein collided with the rear of a parked night-soil wagon. Both vehicles were compromised. Offender deserted the scene in his clattering vehicle before authorities arrived. Some hours later, from a side-street in North Sydney, accompanied by fellow revellers from the Castlecrag function, Stein stole a car matching the make and colour of his own buckled sedan.

At a boat ramp near Balls Head the second, ill-gotten vehicle was soon relieved of its front bumper bar, its radio and the right forward mudguard. The following day, these items were observed affixed to Stein's car.

Before week's end, however, offender presented himself sober and remorseful, accompanied by a solicitor, at Central Street Station.

Resides in St Ives. Has no known criminal associates, the cohort of Castlecrag sots notwithstanding.

Horton Godfrey Baird, alias **Godfrey Horton,** alias **Harold "The Bard" Godfrey**

25 years; 5 ft 5 in; complexion fair; hair light-brown & curly; eyes hazel; inclined to dress "flash", with a penchant for bright colours.

A thick purple 'boxer's scar' over the right eye; two razor-slash scars on the left cheek.

Torso and arms are festooned with tattoos: angel head, "MOTHER" on right upper arm; scroll around right forearm; snake and eagle on left upper arm; dagger, skull, heart, "DEATH BEFORE DISHONOUR" and scroll around left forearm; dagger, heart and "TRUE LOVE PENNY" on left upper chest.

A pigeon-toed shuffler. Ungoverned squint in right eye. Native of Newtown. Occasional labourer.

Assailant, hotel "barber", housebreaker, gas meter meddler & motor cycle thief.

Case study:

> Once caught a train from Bathurst to Sydney Central Station and booked into a Pitt St commercial traveller's hotel. Overnight, while his room-mates were sleeping, offender fiddled each of their wallets, removed a good portion of their money and secreted these gleanings behind the cistern in the shared hallway toilet. Next morning, in town, offender

spent some money on clothing. Four hours later he returned to the hotel, gathered the last remnants of the hidden cash, stole a motor cycle from the street, then rode it to Braidwood and milked fuel from a parked lorry, next retreated to Yass where he made rendezvous with a female consort before attending a dance at a village in the environs. An official at the function took the offender to task regarding lewd behavior on the dancefloor. At the end of proceedings offender made fresh agitation with the official and broke a bottle of beer on the crown of the man's head, thereby fracturing the skull. The motor cycle carried offender and consort fast back into Sydney where, with a man named Tom Butt, they burgled a room at a King's Cross residential. (Note: here they effected entry by scraping away putty and removing a window pane.) A suitcase stuffed with clothing was taken from the rooms. Next door was a boarding-house with a dozen old gas meters, the coin-dole variety. Each of these was bent open and relieved of its holdings.

Since his recent release from custody, offender was last seen on a bicycle in the subway near McDondaldtown train station.

Offender is a "bodgie" type of lair, an incorrigible liar, inimical to work. Consorts with other bodgie types and sundry ne'er-do-wells and cadgers.

Ditto the accomplice Tom Butt: dissolute, shifty.

Information for Vigilance by all Officers

A reward for the arrest of Chi Fung Wong has been increased, by the Vacuum Oils and Gasket Company, to £150.

Long face, artificial teeth, throws his feet outward when walking. A map of Australia tattooed on his chest.

George Andrew Arthur   alias **Arthur Georgeson**

45 years. 5 feet 9 inches. Swarthy complexion. Hair dark brown with grey pepper. Eyes brown flecked with gold. Squint in left eye, especially under bright light.

Stammers when excited. May carry a splash of black blood.

A birth-mark on right forearm.

Tattoo of a horse-shoe around horsehead plus a cap and a whip on right bicep; bird, heart and "MOTHER" on left upper arm.

Labourer; garbage tosser; "greasy spoon" cook. Suffers from lumbago and irritable spirits.

House breaker.

Case study:

> After committing a house-robbery in Bowral, netting £2000 worth of goods and storing them in a motor-vehicle which he had purloined in Concord, Arthur could not resist a vacant premises in Mittagong. (This, on the return trip to Sydney.) Masturbated there in a laundry drawer and left excreta on the floor. A neighbour noticed offender quitting the premises, with front and back seat and trunk of car overloaded. By telephone, this neighbour notified local police who coordinated an interception which culminated, after a siren-chase, on the

western highway near Petersham. All goods were seized at this juncture and were soon returned to their owners. When placed in a cell at Central Street Station, offender stole spectacles from a sleeping fellow-prisoner, broke the lenses from the frames and used the glass edges to cut his left and right wrists, in a futile attempt to be transferred to hospital. No other self-abuse has been reported since the failure of this ruse.

Released recently on licence.

Description of a Man, NAME UNKNOWN

Physical features undetermined.

Case study:

> In Mascot at 2.15 am last Thursday, January 24, an unidentified offender engaged Albert Walter Brennan, a taxi-driver residing at 12 Monarch Drive, San Souci, to convey him to Matraville. On arrival at Matraville, offender instructed Mr Brennan to make a detour to the tram terminus on Botany Rd. Approaching the terminus, offender produced a revolver and demanded keys to the cab. Mr Brennan handed over the keys but at the same time grabbed the revolver and attempted to climb over the front seat to "grapple and pummel" the offender. During the struggle, Mr Brennan was pistol-whipped aside the head, kicked in the face and stomped on the throat.
>
> Mr Brennan extricated himself from the cab and limped toward the offender, who had looked to make escape. Offender turned, brandishing the gun, approached Mr Brennan and pumped a shot into each of the victim's knees, before resuming control of the cab and leaving Mr Brennan prone and bleeding in a culvert.
>
> The cab was subsequently found abandoned in Marrickville, four unused bullets and two shells discarded in the back seat.

Weeks after the event, Mr Brennan remembered that the man wore a workingman's cap of stained navy-blue serge.

Richard Maurice Bosquet — soon to be released

33 years; 5ft 8in; slight build; fair complexion and hair; green eyes; good teeth; sharp face, small ears, dimpled chin and smile; long tapered fingers.

"True Love" tattooed on right outside upper arm; red rose on left breast over his heart. Very softly spoken; always wears hat cocked on the back of his head.

Case studies:

> Committed indecent assault on a kneeling male person named Walter Battherham in lavatories of Wynyard rail station. Convicted to eighteen months' labour. Soon to be released amongst decent citizens again.
>
> On an earlier occasion, offender was discovered on a grass border in a street in Darlinghurst at 3.00am on a summer's night, engaged in the act of satisfying the unnatural desires of himself and a youth known as Mattison by placing the latter's penis in his mouth. (Mattison was also convicted of a commensurate charge. Mattison was released after six months' hard labour.)

Offender is an individual unchaste and worthless of clemency, and since imprisonment for the Batterham outrage and following reported depraved activities in the gaol, the offender is now most likely rapidly approaching complete and permanent degradation.

On release, he may go to Coonabarabran where his brother resides.

Owen Masters Jones — ACQUITTED OF CHARGES

49 years; stout build; dark complexion; black wavy hair oiled and brushed back. Large surgical scar on right side of abdomen.

"Dear Mother" tattooed on left forearm, three different nude women (including a black girl) on right upper arm and down the forearm to wrist.

When walking, usually has right hand in pocket and head turned to left side. Addicted to drink.
Associates with reprobates in The Haymarket, named Murphy, Silk, Sidden and Maloney.

Acquitted of having carnally known his own tender step-daughter, Margaret Marie Evans, 15 years old. (Officers are advised to pledge continuous vigilance.)

John Raymond Cozier   alias **Raymond John Cox**

41 years; 5ft 11in; sunburned complexion; blond hair and brown eyes; wiry, athletic physique; large scar on right shin; red welt under left eye; all the fingers of the right hand have been broken and bent sometime in the far past; wears horn-rimmed brown spectacles.

A native of Balmain.

A shipwright and harbour pilot. Plausible false pretender.

Case study:

> Having purchased a 120-foot boat, offender sought subscribers to a syndicate intending to develop a 24,000-acre coffee plantation in coastal New Guinea as well as sea-farming rights to purported lobster hatcheries in waters adjacent to that coast. Offender presented a (bogus) prospectus guaranteeing immediate sales of frozen produce to American companies and traders in Hong Kong.
>
> Numerous investors committed £1000 per-person shares to the enterprises, grossing for offender a large store of cash many times in excess of the price of the vessel. (Offender had guaranteed monthly bonuses and plush travel benefits to shareholders.)
>
> In command of a small company of men, women and children, offender left Sydney for northern waters, aboard the 120-foot

vessel, towing two smaller craft said to be fitted out for lobster capture and preservation.

On a night with no moon, offshore north of Brisbane, offender deserted the boat and decamped for the shore, taking the tow-boats and leaving entire unskilled company to their fate on the mother ship. (As good fortune dictated, the mother ship drifted in to shore near Gladstone, where the distressed crew were disembarked, embarrassed but unharmed.)

In the following months, unapprehended, offender purchased a smaller boat in Townsville, deploying the same subscription-based caper, garnering a new range of investors, promising a thriving fishing and tourism venture on the Great Barrier Reef. Having secured plentiful funds, offender absconded straight to New Guinea. Was last sighted in Port Moresby. May have re-located to Singapore or Hong Kong. Unlikely to return to Sydney. Officers are advised to maintain correspondence with foreign police bureaux, especially in the near Orient.

Always appears plausible and persuasive. An accomplished navigator and sailor. A loner. Appears to be equally appealing to men and to women. No known underworld associates.

Heinrich Albert Fischer   alias "**Hooka**"

45 years; 5ft 8 in; thickset build; medium complexion; fair hair; blue eyes; top joints of three fingers missing on left hand; burn scars on fingers of right hand and along inside right forearm and upper arm; shrapnel scars on left hip and leg.

Native of Katoomba. Labourer. Thief.

Case study:

> Under cover of night, offender broke into abattoir yards in Katoomba. Slaughtered three pigs and hauled them, in a stolen lorry, to his brother's house in Petersham where he drained and cleaned them and suspended them till offering them to suspicious local butchers the following morning. (Bloody lorry found abandoned in Tempe.) Has not returned to his Katoomba abode.

May have decamped now to farmland in the Central Highlands of NSW.

Boris Nevis Bede

33 years; 5ft 10in; slender build; fair complexion and hair; hazel eyes; chipped front teeth in upper jaw.

A scar in the right eye-brow, the result of a bashing.

Is said to speak French and Spanish and consorts often with foreigners. Enjoys the company of sailors from Asia.

A teacher of youths at a private Catholic school. Sexual pervert.

Case studies:

> Indecent assault, in the offender's own home, on a male person, Stanley Duke, 22 years. Duke then returned the assault, several times , according to testimony; unnatural offences were repeatedly visited upon each other on consecutive days in house, park and bus station.
>
> On the occasion of a previous conviction 10 months ago (for an assault on one Ambrose Andrew Gleeson, 21 of Glebe), offender was bound over for Good Behaviour across a period of three years, instructed to appear and receive sentence if caught and convicted for new outrages during that period. Offender was instructed also to enter an institution approved by the Clerk of the Peace, for treatment of perversion and to forward to the Clerk, at intervals of three months, a medical certificate as to his present physical, medical, emotional

and mental conditions. It transpires that offender has lapsed from these duties and has re-offended, this time with Duke, whom offender has clearly led into perdition and who is now undergoing the same lenient first sanctions that offender has just failed.

Offender is presently on remand awaiting prosecution with a view to incarceration in Long Bay or Goulburn.

Ilaria Maria Brancatisano

32 years; 5ft 3 in; slender build; olive complexion; black hair; brown eyes; scar on each side of jaw; blind in right eye; deaf in right ear; native speaker of Italian; poor English expression.

Housekeeper and lodging-house proprietor. Manslaughterer.

Case study:

> Whilst residing in a house in Enmore, offender took in a man and his wife as lodgers, full bed and board. After some months the man entered offender's room one night when offender was ill in bed and lodger took intercourse with her despite her protestation.
>
> One morning several weeks later, offender went into victim's room armed with a tomahawk, which she had purchased the previous day, and savaged him as he lay in bed, striking him fifteen blows about the head and shoulders, knocking him to the floor and dispatching him to death with one deep chop to the forehead.
>
> After washing herself and changing clothes, offender went to the local Police Station to report all details of the matter.

After serving four years' hard labour, convicted for manslaughter, offender has recently been released.

Thought to be residing now in a boarding-house in Potts Point or Kings Cross.

Rolf Henry Herbertson

30 years; 5ft 7in; a native of England; North Country accent; fresh complexion, brown hair, blue eyes; large circular scars on front of both knees; ears protrude handle-like.

A labourer on Hickson Road wharves. Sexual offender and shoplifter.

Case study:

> Stood on the steps in a hallway leading to a business college in the City where he exposed his person to a girl on her way to a class; offender then walked to a nearby retail store and stole four pairs of green socks.

Frequents the City, Darlinghurst, Potts Point and Kings Cross.

Mavis Patricia Hollister alias **Grantham**
alias **Patricia Masterton** alias **Mavis Patrick**

26 years; 5ft 4in, plump build; sallow complexion; brown curly hair; goiter scar under chin; moles under left eye and over right eye.

"I love my husband Bill" tattooed on left upper arm.

A native of Erskineville; domestic labourer and chore-runner.

Embezzler, boarding-house "barber" and window breaker. Adopting a series of aliases, offender finds employment in wealthy households and decamps soon after with spoils.

Case Study:

On October 23 1954, offender pretended to be a new night nurse at a convalescent home in Blakehurst where she stole a wristlet watch, cash and clothing from patients; then walked out of the institution. A week later, with Ruby Edna Jackson, stole two handbags from a display in a city emporium; both were arrested when leaving the building. After escaping whilst on escort from Strathfield Railway Station, offender abandoned Mrs Jackson to her fates and travelled to Katoomba where, the following day, she smashed the display window of a jeweller's shop and stole a number of gent's watches and crystal scapulae and brooches. On this occasion she was dressed as a man.

Two years earlier, offender hatched a scheme to secure insurance compensation by setting fire to her house. But almost immediately, the blaze was doused by a thunderstorm. No compensation ensued. And ten months' hard labour were endured for the fraudulent scheme.

Was once ejected from a church for a loud, blasphemous utterance.

A daring type who associates with "bodgies", criminals and prostitutes in the City.

May have decamped now to Queensland. Or Western Australia. Seems never bereft of a scheme or a fool who will play partner to her ruse. Appears to be strongly attractive for men, despite a bearing and grooming that would suggest otherwise.

Henry Edward Wallinghurst   alias "The Birch"

51 years; 6ft 1in; ruddy complexion; russet hair; hazel eyes; scar on right side of neck; large scar along outside of left leg; multiple scars on each buttock; in habit of shaving all body hair; a native of England.

A fireman, retired due to injuries. Sexual pervert.

Case studies:

> Offender has committed a number of offences in the Castlecrag, Middle Harbour, French's Forest areas, particularly in nature reserves; usually appearing in front of secluded picnic groups naked and demanding that they whip him with a cane and commit indecent assaults upon his person. Thus the offender has become known in the district as "The Birch".

Albert James Missenden

33 years; 5ft 8in; dark complexion; brown hair and eyes; prematurely bald; fractured skull palpable just above the base of the neck; appears to suffer chest trouble. A labourer and bricklayer's help, sometimes a wheeler, sometimes a slurry jockey.

Razor slasher.

Case study:

> Separated from his wife, offender called at her home one night and asked to be admitted. Wife refused entreaties, but compromised by allowing offender to speak to her at the front window. After some minutes of conversation offender drew a razor from trouser pocket and slashed at the wife, causing a sickle-shaped wound in her cheek which needed seventeen stitches. Offender next fled to a nearby park and attempted to take own life by cutting his throat, and although wound demanded twenty-three stitches, offender failed to pass away.
>
> Previously convicted also for attempted extortion of a starting-price bookmaker, having threatened outrage on the man's daughter.

Convicted to three years' hard labour for inflicting GBH; extra conviction (three years' hard labour) for attempting the suicide. Recently released.

May have gone to Wollongong, where his old grandmother resides.

Albert Rothwell McAdam

5ft 7in; sallow complexion; dark brown hair and eyes; fastidiously dressed in navy-blue pin-striped suit.

Heart and scroll displaying "True Love Mother Always" tattooed on left breast above heart. A red birth-mark stain, like the splash of cruel scald, on right palm and wrist.

A native of Victoria; a boarding-house chef.

Sexual Pervert.

Recently released after 6 months' hard labour for mutual indecent assaults with a male person. See below.

Case studies:

> Made the acquaintance of Henry Clyde Bailey (1955 Photobook 217, page 23) in the city one summer night and retired to Hyde Park where they put hands on each other, leading to acts of indecency reported by a romancing couple (man and woman) already installed in the bower that the men had come to.
>
> After accosting the couple, the men retired to a room at the Peoples' Palace and there submitted each other to loud, depraved acts, causing management intervention and premature eviction.

Several days later, offender and Bailey, in the company of a group of other men, retired from a hotel in Erskineville and broke into the cold-room of a butcher shop nearby. When arrested soon after, all the men concurred that they had entered the premises intent on sexual orgy.

(Offender has previously been reported for behaving amorously toward a 75-year-old matron in Waterloo. No crime was proven in this instance, but police left offender in no doubt he should desist and decamp.)

Outrage perpetrated by a man, Name Unknown

November 17th, 1956. Offender indecently exposed himself to Millicent Mae Howie (residing at 15A Hartigan Terrace, North Sydney) in a railway carriage between Wynyard and Town Hall stations.

35 to 40 years; 5ft 4 or 5in; thin build; flushed complexion; dirty grey flannel trousers, sports coat and olive-green felt hat; carried a small brown leather attaché case, which was deployed as a "device" in his performance.

Cases Closed

Tempe. Cook's River Reserve. Clarence Edward Aspinall (56 years) has murdered Jessica Jane Charleston (21 years) alongside the Cook's River. Offender shot victim multiple times with a crank-loading pea-rifle and then hanged himself in a tree that cants over the water. The bodies were found by schoolboys riding bicycles. An outrage betrayed by its own stench.

Waterloo, 14 Cope Street. Fearing that death had chosen to neglect her, the old widow Abigail Cameron (88 years) sent her daughter to the markets and then took matters into her hands.

Vexed by their inability to blast open a safe in the premises of the Royal Motor Association in Pitt Street, the City, offenders set a new bigger charge which blew the entire office right out to nowhere. Ditto themselves.

Nameless offenders have set an excessive explosion in a Redfern butcher's shop, casting mincemeat across Botany Road and onto windows all around. Offenders' own offal was among the ordure.

Rushcutter's Bay Stadium. An assailant has doused a young woman's petticoats in kerosene and set them alight. Offender was apprehended at scene. A citizens' arrest. Trial set for February 1958.

A note has been received at Central Street Station explaining that an unnamed man has been paid to defile the daughter of the Mayor. The Mayor claims to have no daughter.

With a large paintbrush and pail, someone has daubed 'DUST MENZIES' in four-foot high script on the front wall of the Australian Youth Hotel. Publican has not registered a complaint. Therefore, no action required.

Newly Arrived Malefactors

An interstate criminal about whom little is known. Presently masquerading as a casual dance instructor in The Haymarket and Petersham. Immaculate appearance, often sporting hat, gloves and silk scarf.

An Englishman frequenting taverns and restaurants in Vaucluse and Dover Heights. Pencil-thin moustache. A swagger to his gait. But he is such a dandy in many gestures, that he veers to the effeminate. Claims to be a long-distance aeroplane pilot. And a graduate of Cambridge.

An unrecognised newcomer. 20 years old. Lifts overcoats and jackets from foyers of dance halls while patrons occupy the floor or are otherwise engaged. Is wearing a different jacket or coat every time he is espied. Inclined to dress "flash".

An ex-constable, disgraced, of the Victorian Police, poised and plausible, but addicted to drink and prone to false representation.

Assorted Malefactor Quirks
(A "glossary" for noting when interviewing or observing culprits roundabout)

Addicted to risk; foolhardy and boastful.

Dismissed from the Police Force, the Army, the Navy, the Airforce.

An esoteric medical doctor (or a pretender as such).

Ditto a false lawyer, a motor mechanic, a Councillor or Justice of the Peace.

Talkative to a fault.

A scoundrel, but plausible, even compelling or empathetic.

Walking stooped; walking quickly; walking with arms extended forcefully downwards, the fingers all twitching; arms probing forward; or thrust to the back; a leg swinging out away, with a shuffle, or a slide or a glide or a jig; evincing any characteristics of some identifiable animal – a cat or a bear, a rat or a snake, jumpy like a monkey, baleful as a hound.

The mouth always cosseting a cigarette , or a pipe, or tobacco wadded up to masticate and spit. Or snuff up the nose.

Suntanned appearance; or a sallow complexion; or swarthy, ruddy, blotched-red or freckled, birth-marked or acne-scarred; perfectly unblemished; peaches & cream; an apple-cheeked glow; or blue-lipped when cold.

Birthmarks – location, colour and configuration. Ditto any scars. By accident? On purpose?

Peculiar stance? E.G. hands clasped or not; arms crossed, arms akimbo; upright stance; inclined to lean on walls, door-jambs or posts.

Condition of teeth; face fat or thin; double chin; square-jawed or otherwise?

Number and condition of fingers. Ditto the ears, toes, eyes and brows.

Speaking with an accent, be it false and "put on", or actual from a homeland.

Erect carriage; or slovenly; or stooped; canted left or right at the hips; head up or down; silent or garrulous; shoulders square, or round, or ill-balanced; a bobbing, loping or gliding comportment; a limp or a swagger; note the entire bodily alignment – tensile or slack, straight-lined and sharp-angled or bulbous and soft.

"Bodgie" type of hoon, associating with young rascals and making them worse; lurking in milk bars, billiard parlours, cinema stalls, two-up schools; assembling in beach suburbs; or rivals from inner-west – Zetland, Darlington, Mascot, McDonaldtown.

Nose slightly askew; or upturned: or slavered flat; winey red; Roman; unbroken; negroid, aquiline, Levantine; pointed, blunt, nobby or flared.

Scars, be they X-inscribed, or sickle-curved or puncture-starred; on what parts of the body; scraped, burned or whipped; razor-slashed; convex; concave; made by a hand, an animal or a machine; a surgical scar; the result of assault; an accident; self-abuse; or disdain.

Likely to puff out left side of face when fabulating or dissembling.

Spattered with shrapnel scars – specify which body parts.

A cast in which eye; a squint; a crossed or wandering or wall eye. (Even if unafflicted, do the eyes appear dreamy, or deadly, or dull or disconsolate?)

Servile to drink; enslaved to Benzedrine, aspirin, muscle relaxant; addicted to cocaine and other derivatives of morphine.

Pursuing dubious income, not necessarily illegal – E.G. a model for an artist; begging with an infant; collection and re-sale of dumped roadside rubbish; minding a car-parking space for a profligate client; foraging and selling edible native vegetation or market-stall refuse.

Subject to involuntary gestures with hands, fingers, shoulders or facial expressions.

Unable to look a man or a woman in the eye.

The fingers on each hand – are they bent out of shape? How many and which? Count the thumbs in these descriptions.

Nose pointing left; nose pointing right; flattened at bridge; devoid of soft cartilage.

High forehead; or a low brow; pointed jaw; receding chin.

Smart or dapper guises; athletic appearance; or slovenly slow to rouse and rise and walk; inability to speak up; inability to quieten down.

Skiting of unusual prowess: E.G. as a crooner, a songwriter, a fondler and copulator, a horse or dog trainer, a floral arranger, a dancer, a bushman, a comforter of the sick, a hospital troubadour, a guardian angel to children.

A scheming backstreet youth masquerading as a country lad.

Chest trouble; eye trouble; lumbago; arthritis in knee, hip or neck; nerves unappreciative of din, stench or glare.

Fear of birds, cockroaches, snakes, spiders, bananas, coffee grounds and damp tea leaves, chiming clocks, soft putty around glass within wooden window frames, a door with no lock.

Freckles on face, shoulders, flanks, forehead, the backs of the hands; cankers; moles; contusions that are not scars or strap marks; ruddiness; pallor; shingles; prickly heat.

Tattoos

Lion and boxer on left forearm; elephant on right forearm; woman and heart on right leg; handshake, woman, boxer, woman's head and scroll on left leg; Donald Duck, heart, scroll, star and two wrestlers on chest. All on one man.

Anchor and rope, ship and "U.S.N." on left forearm; "V E R A" on fingers of left hand, "M.Y." on right; Maltese cross on back of left hand; bird and "My Patricia" on chest. All on one man.

Popeye and a dancing girl on left and right bicep.

A waratah on the left breast.

"L E F T" and "R I G H T" on fingers (and thumb) of relevant hands.

"T R U E" and "L O V E" on fingers of left and right hand.

"Death before Dishonour" on right upper arm.

A Colt 45 revolver on right upper arm.

A Colt 45 revolver in holster on right hip.

Stump, bird and snake wrapped around the left forearm.

A map of Tasmania on top of the heart.

A map of Tasmania on pubis above penis.

"Sailor's Grave", sinking battleship, "Last Salute", laurels and heart and anchor all along the right arm.

"E D I T H" on fingers and thumb of left hand.

"Ruin of Man" in a scroll on right upper arm.

Chinaman and dagger on right upper arm; hula girl on left upper arm.

Skull in pilot's helmet over a propeller on left upper arm.

"Beatrice" on back of right hand; rising sun, "Tel Aviv" and "MOTHER" on right forearm; sword all along left arm.

Bucking horse, rider and "King of the Ring" on right forearm.

"AIF NX180192" on back of left hand.

"Australia 1939" on left upper arm.

"Mother", a nude girl, "Oh Boy!" on right upper arm.

Woman in helmet plus "Britannia" on centre of chest.

Horse head, scroll and butterfly on back of right hand; "Dad" on right forearm; eagle and cowboy on chest; ship on abdomen. All on one man.

Dagger in heart on left upper arm; rising sun and crossed swords on right upper arm.

"Margaret", "Marie" and "Eve" along the left arm; "Nell", "Mum" and Catholic sacred heart along the right arm.

On middle of chest, a heart inscribed with "Joy" over-written with a large black "X".

"Roy", "Hi Babe" on fingers; "True" on back of right hand; "Mother", "Dot" and "Saints" on right forearm; "Nanna" on right upper arm; dagger on left forearm; arrow in heart plus "S.O.S." on left upper arm; cross bones and anchor on left shoulder-blade; skull and propeller on chest; triangle in square on left upper leg. All on one man.

Missing Persons

Douglas Campbell Nettleford

46 years; 5ft 10in; medium build; suntanned complexion; thick wavy brown hair turning grey at the temples.

Left his Mascot home in the early morning on Friday, March 24th, stepping on to a tram with only his bill-fold and a freshly laundered bath-towel. Possibly wearing a blue serge suit and a Homburg hat. (His clothing is made by a London firm which post-delivers.)

May be deep in a drinking spree. Or sequestered with some quiet woman unknown to his family.

Person presenting inquiry: Rosalind Abigail Nettleford.

Special Inquiry Registered by the Queensland Police Searching for Edna Rosalene Nixon

Registered as missing by her employer, the Queensland State Public Service.

On February 11th, Miss Nixon obtained special leave of absence from Brisbane to visit relatives in Mackay, but investigations show that she did not visit there. She was driven to the Railway Station by her Work Supervisor on the afternoon of the 11th. But was not actually seen on platform and it is doubtful that she was ever aboard the train. Miss Nixon is 30 years old; 5ft 6in or 7in; medium build with rather well-covered hips; dark brown hair very nearly black, waved and dressed close to the head; striking blue eyes; freckled face which is often applied with ample make-up to hide what she has been known to name as 'blemishes'; oftentimes anaemic in appearance; her manicured fingernails are short and may be painted a bright red; upper jaw is supplied with several artificial teeth; was wearing a gold oblong wristlet watch and a three-stone diamond ring with a claw setting of yellow gold; may be wearing a dark blue dress and a white hat; well educated and bright conversationalist fond of company and dancing. It has been established that she had a sum of £175 in her possession on the day of her disappearance. A search of her room has disclosed that the only clothing that is missing is a dark costume, a white hat, a midnight-blue silk kimono, a pair of pyjamas plus a small brown fibre suitcase. As she was in fine health at the time, in no obvious way despondent, and was avid about her employment, grave fears are entertained for her security.

Jessie Margaret McNamara

17 years old; 5ft 5in; stout build; fair complexion; brown hair matching her eyes; three artificial teeth in upper front jaw; recent sickle-shaped scar above her left eye; inclined to be pigeon-toed; shy, wary and reticent, tending to hide facial expressions in her long curly hair. Last sighted wearing a black tailor-made costume, white sailor-blouse, fawn stockings and black suede shoes.

A native of New Zealand.

House worker for a doctor's family.

Did not return home from an after-hours assignation on June 17th. May be in the company of a girl who sings on a Sydney Harbour Show Boat.

Person presenting inquiry: Valerie Margaret McNamara.

Dorothy Hetherington

16 years old; 4ft 10in; medium build and complexion; dark bobbed hair over brown eyes; excellent teeth. Speaks quickly when nervous, evincing a slight lisp.

Last seen at Marrickville. May be located in the company of one Malcolm Merton, 19 years old, who is a larrikin, lecherous and an occasional labourer hailing from Maitland.

Person presenting inquiry: James Percival Hetherington.

Robert Michael Hartigan

16 years old; 5ft 8in; thin & bony; gawky & maladroit; fair complexion and hair; pimpled skin blemishes; blue eyes; normal teeth. Wearing grey trousers, grey sports coat, soft white shirt and black shoes.

Left home with no provocation or warning on May 1st, riding a red Malvern Star bicycle. Believed to have gone to Bega in the company of Ralph Gordon (19 years old), also riding a bicycle (thought to be a Speedwell). May seek employment on a boat.

Person presenting inquiry: Cedric James Hartigan.

Alfred Bede Chidlington

16 years; slight build; fair wavy hair and complexion; grey eyes, the right of which waters in glare of full sunlight; dressed in blue suit and tan shoes.

Left home in Short St, Waterloo on 23rd June, riding a black and white bicycle, carrying a spare suit of clothing, £5 and a tennis racquet. On June 26 his mother (Agnes Alice Chidlington) received a letter stating that her son had been taken for a ride and would not be harmed.

Person presenting inquiry: Agnes Alice Chidlington

Joan McEhlone (possibly using surname of Bullen)

17 years; 5ft 4in; medium build; dressed in black coat, black slacks and white sandals; dark complexion, long dark hair, brown eyes.

Left home in Pitt St, Redfern on September 17th stating an intention to run away to Yass. Carrying a small Australian terrier, light brown, in a canvas satchel. May be in the company of Daniel Kevin Pollock, 17 years old, believed to be a rouseabout at Randwick Racing Stables.

Person presenting inquiry: Esme Bullen.

Vincent Moncrieff Cobbs

27 years; 5ft 11in; thin build; dark complexion and very dark wavy hair; clean shaven and fastidious about grooming; blue eyes; wearing a pencil-striped navy suit and white shirt with a thin stripe; tan elastic-sided boots; oblong wrist-watch of yellow-gold.

Failed to return home from employment at Tavistock Solicitors firm, December 19th. Has been bleak and despondent and may be suffering loss of memory and impaired sense of direction.

Person presenting inquiry: Oona Mavis O'Toole (19 years old).

Hillary Katherine Bailey

35 years; 5ft 5in, thin build, sallow complexion, auburn hair, blue eyes, artificial teeth, horn-rimmed glasses. Wearing a red frock with a large brooch set with coloured stones; maroon-coloured overcoat adorned by large fur collar, dark tan shoes, thin gold wedding ring.

Left home at Henderson Rd, Alexandria in early morning of May 2nd. May be in the company of a man named Gordon Gilbert; or may have entered a hospital for treatment as she is of a nervous disposition and has recently had to grieve the passing of both parents.

Person presenting inquiry: Edna Margaret Cunningham (22 years old).

Ronald Terence O'Shea

11 years, big for his age; fair complexion and hair; blue eyes; small scar under bottom lip; wearing dark brown shorts, green Guernsey, green tie; black shoes and socks; no hat.

Left home at 13 Union St, Newtown on May 13th; accompanied by black poodle dog and bouncing a multi-coloured ball.

Person presenting inquiry: Esme Alice O'Shea (28 years old).

Amy Elspeth Darnley

35 years; 5ft 5in; bobbed, fair hair and ruddy complexion; hazel eyes; slightly paralysed in right arm and leg; walks with a limp; wearing navy-blue overcoat, flesh-coloured stockings, black shoes and no hat.

Left home in 16 Dalmeny St, Rosebery, July 25th, having installed a large pot of mutton stew simmering on the stove-top.

Person presenting inquiry: Elizabeth Ann Balantyne, (67 years old), co-habitant with the missing person.

Allan Barnet Forester

15 years; 5ft 6in, medium build, fair complexion and hair; a blue-purple bruise around the right eye; wearing grey trousers, lumber jacket, grey socks and black shoes (the uniform of a messenger boy).

Left home at 19 Laverton St, Willoughby on August 1st, riding a bicycle with the frame sanded back to the metal. May be gone to the Hawkesbury River in search of new employment as an oyster-setter or skiff pilot; may be sleeping in caves about the river shore there.

Person presenting inquiry: Elaine Mary Forester (33 years old).

Kay Kidlington   alias **May Millington**

26 years; 5ft 6in; medium build; fair complexion, fair bobbed wavy hair; wearing a pink Fuji silk frock, coat with a brown fur collar and black buckle shoes; carrying a black alligator-clipped handbag.

Left house in 16 Cope St, Redfern on April 1st. Had been speaking on telephone to persons unknown, discussing a debt of some kind as well as "shame and humiliation". Fears are held for the safety of this woman.

Person presenting inquiry: Oliver Anderson Smyth (35 years old).

Patience Hope Wallace

19 years old; stout build; fair complexion and hair; light blue eyes, bright red lipstick; wearing a black frock with large white dots, a black woollen pull-over with a wide white woven waistband and brown shoes with no socks or stockings.

Left her home in 37 Mitchell Road, Alexandria on 28th May. May be in the company of Alexander Callaghan, a flash dandy procurer hailing from Kings Cross.

Person presenting inquiry: Maisie Maude Wallace (17 years old).

Elwyn Oscar Arlington

11 years old; thin build; fair complexion; brown hair and eyes; wearing a grey suit with short trousers, a brown raincoat, grey and gold socks, black shoes and a felt hat. The uniform of a schoolboy.

May be doubling on a blue bicycle with a person unknown. Left home with person unknown 14th July. Carrying a small brown fibre attaché case and cloth bag full of apples.

Person presenting inquiry: Fanny Muriel Arlington (35 years old).

Grace Nellie Harvey

22 years; 5ft 4in; thin, wiry build; dark complexion and black hair; good serviceable teeth; may be dressed in a red overcoat, black shoes and a black hat.

Left home in Chalmers St Surry Hills on 23rd July, accompanied by her children Walter (3 years) and Donald (5 months). May go to Gerringong via Wollongong, or out far west to Wee Waa and stations beyond.

Person presenting inquiry: Albert Gordon Edwards (48 years old).

Mabel Gwen Perry

50 years; 5ft 8in, stout build; fresh complexion, apple cheeks; light brown curly hair; grey eyes; preponderance of artificial teeth; horn-rimmed spectacles; inveterate smoker; has a hearty, stentorous laugh and may be somewhat mental.

Last observed January 3rd at Cosmopolitan Hotel, public bar, City. May be in the company of Jack Landers, 32 years, 5ft 8in, well built, Roman nose, a labourer, gambler and inebriant thought to be currently "on a tear".

Person presenting inquiry: Augustus Campbell (32 years old), no fixed abode, last seen in public lobby of People's Palace, Pitt St, City.

Alfred Gordon Tenney   alias **Alfie "Cadger" Tenner**

27 years; 5ft 10in, medium build, dark complexion and hair which is thick and wavy; chalky blue eyes; may be wearing dark trousers, navy-blue striped blazer, grey tweed overcoat, black shoes and socks.

Absconded from Riverina Welfare Farm last Friday September 7th. May be seeking re-attachment with a Sydney-side sweetheart. Or revenge. (Recent correspondence found in pieces under his bed at Welfare Farm.)

Officers are advised to search inner-west hostels and churchyards. Person presenting inquiry: Chief Warden, Riverina Welfare Farm.

Hazel Alice Standish and Alrene Carruthers

Standish is 15 years, 5ft 6in, strikingly well built; medium complexion; light-brown curly hair; may be wearing a reddish-coloured dress with a blue topcoat and matching blue felt hat plus fawn-coloured stockings and black buckled shoes.

Carruthers is 17 years, 5ft 9in, tall and very thin and flat-chested; olive complexion; straight, thin mousey-brown hair cut as if in a cake basin; wearing a grey overcoat and brown hat, fawn-coloured stockings and lace-up black shoes. Slow in her thinking, prone to be hoodwinked, and often used unpleasantly by predatory men.

Both are Wards of the State and are carrying light suitcases.

Person presenting inquiry: Ivy Agnes Simpkins, Public Servant of State.

Joseph Cedric Mandible

28 years; 5ft 6in, stout build (12 stones); dark complexion and dark crinkled hair oiled into order; blue eyes, usually inflamed; large sharp pointed nose; large mouth with thick lips sometimes ulcerated; fat pasty face; one gold-capped tooth in upper front jaw; usually clean-shaven; "Sheriff Girl" tattooed on left forearm. Small half-closed grey eyes tattooed on left breast over heart; a wharf labourer and hoister.

Left wife and family in Annandale, who suspect him to be living now with a stout woman and her thin girl-child. Last heard of in Glebe but also reported in Forbes. Believed to be a thrilling singer; may have taken off for Victoria.

Person presenting inquiry: Ivy Anne Mandible (29 years old).

Angelina Caputo

30 years, but looks younger; 5ft 4in, slim build, fair complexion and hair; blue eyes; dresses in a fashionable, up-to-date style (is a native of Italy).

Left home in Short St, Annandale on May 19th, accompanied by her three children aged 13, 9 & 8. Thought to have gone to some remote part of the country, but perhaps a grimmer escapade has unfolded.

Person presenting inquiry: Giovanni Caputo (45 years old).

Martin O'Bannion   alias **Martin Bannister**   alias **Ben Martin**

21 years; stout build; dark complexion; black curly hair; brown eyes; one tooth missing in front. Wearing light grey trousers, check shirt, dark grey coat and a brown cap. Of quiet, pleasant disposition; is said to be almost always smiling. Frequents the City and the Municipal Markets. Hangs about with a gang, who use him for amusement.

A newsboy and sometime market rouseabout, he is subject to fits.

Left his home in Waterloo on 15th March. May be "riding the rattlers" on lines west of Lithgow.

Person presenting inquiry: Agnes Esma Bannister (39 years old).

Vera Margaret Mainwaring

17 years; slight build; olive complexion; brown hair and eyes; teeth decayed in front; wearing grey costume, black hat turned off face with white bow in front; fond of the company of sailors.

Left home in 157 Cleveland St Surry Hills on 2nd August. May be in thrall to a more vivacious girl named Peggy.

Person presenting inquiry: Edward Andrew Galbally (17 years).

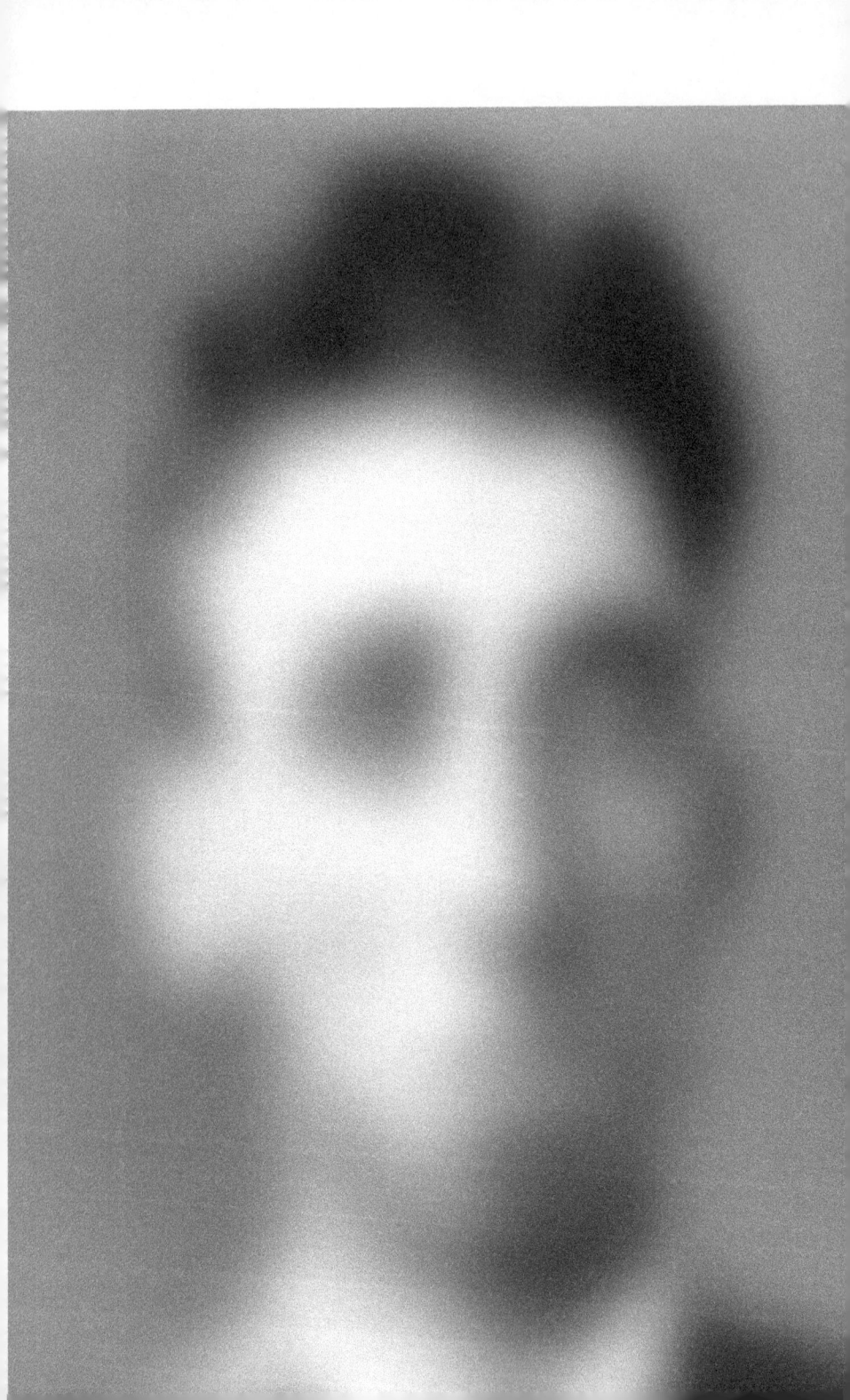

A Note about the Images

The photographic portraits that I found in the junk shop when I apprehended my Register all seemed to want to go with the big book. And it felt proper that I should alter the images in some manner, to make them mine in a way similar to how I had redacted the police texts.

I scanned the originals and then printed the digital files on a heavy matt paper. Using a cotton ball, I rubbed at the edges of the new versions of the portraits and then buffed them a little more lightly all over. This got me halfway to an effect that I wasn't able to prescribe but that I hoped I would recognise when eventually I generated it.

The next step delivered. I overlaid a rubbed portrait with a sheet of trace paper. This brought a ghost out and made it float in some haze that felt partly like oblivion and partly like yearning. What's more, the face was not recognisable now as any particular citizen who once walked the earth. Rather it was some kind of visitant, bringing who-knows-what.

So I trace-veiled every buffed portrait and put the assemblages back on the scanner. Which produced what you see.

www.ingramcontent.com/pod-product-compliance
Lightning Source LLC
Chambersburg PA
CBHW032228080426
42735CB00008B/769